State Dept. of Public Instruction

School Laws of the State of Montana

comprising all the laws in force pertainign to public schools, state educational institutions, school lands and public lands appropriated to the use of the state educational institutions

State Dept. of Public Instruction

School Laws of the State of Montana
comprising all the laws in force pertainign to public schools, state educational institutions, school lands and public lands appropriated to the use of the state educational institutions

ISBN/EAN: 9783337192556

Printed in Europe, USA, Canada, Australia, Japan

Cover: Foto ©Paul-Georg Meister /pixelio.de

More available books at **www.hansebooks.com**

SCHOOL LAWS

OF THE

STATE OF MONTANA

COMPRISING ALL THE LAWS IN FORCE PERTAINING TO PUBLIC
SCHOOLS, STATE EDUCATIONAL INSTITUTIONS, SCHOOL
LANDS AND PUBLIC LANDS APPROPRIATED TO
THE USE OF THE STATE EDUCATIONAL
INSTITUTIONS.

COMPILED AT THE OFFICE OF THE

SUPERINTENDENT OF PUBLIC INSTRUCTION

MAY 1, 1899.

PUBLISHED BY AUTHORITY.

Helena, Montana:
INDEPENDENT PUBLISHING CO.,
State Printers and Binders.
1899.

SCHOOL LAWS

OF THE

STATE OF MONTANA

COMPRISING ALL THE LAWS IN FORCE PERTAINING TO PUBLIC SCHOOLS, STATE EDUCATIONAL INSTITUTIONS, SCHOOL LANDS AND PUBLIC LANDS APPROPRIATED TO THE USE OF THE STATE EDUCATIONAL INSTITUTIONS.

COMPILED AT THE OFFICE OF THE

SUPERINTENDENT OF PUBLIC INSTRUCTION

MAY 1, 1899.

PUBLISHED BY AUTHORITY.

Helena, Montana:
INDEPENDENT PUBLISHING CO.,
State Printers and Binders.
1899.

State of Montana,
Department of Public Instruction.

This Pamphlet contains the School Laws of the State in force to date.

E. A. CARLETON,
Superintendent of Public Instruction.

Helena, Montana, May, 1899.

THIS VOLUME IS STATE PROPERTY

And is for the use of the School Officers of..................School District No........, County of..........................., State of Montana.

School officers on retiring from office, are required by law to deliver this volume, with all other books and documents of an official character, to their successors in office. The Clerk is the proper custodian of this book.

CONTENTS.

PROVISIONS OF THE ENABLING ACT.

	Page
Public Schools	2
Schools Lands	2

CONSTITUTIONAL PROVISIONS.

		Page
Article	V.—The Legislative Department	4
Article	VII.—The Executive Department	4
Article	IX.—Elective Franchise	5
Article	X.—State Institutions	5
Article	XI.—Education	5
Article	XIII.—Public Indebtedness	7
Article	XVII.—Public Lands	8

STATUTORY PROVISIONS.
TITLE III.—EDUCATION.

		Page
Chapter	I.—State Board of Education	9
Chapter	II.—State University of Montana	12
Chapter	III.—School of Mines of Montana	16
Chapter	IV.—Agricultural College of Montana	20
Chapter	V.—State Normal School	22
Chapter	VI.—Public Schools	24
Chapter	VII.—Deaf and Dumb Asylum	79
Chapter	VIII.—Authorizing State Board of Education to Select Land for Educational Institutions	86
Chapter	IX.—Text-books	87
Chapter	X.—University Bond Bill	91
Chapter	XI.—School of Mines Bond Bill	94
Chapter	XII.—Deaf and Dumb Asylum Bond Bill	98
Chapter	XIII.—Forms	108
Article	I.—Superintendent of Public Instruction	24
Article	II.—County Superintendent of Schools	28
Article	III.—School Districts	31
Article	IV.—Election of School Trustees	35
Article	V.—Board of Trustees	45
Article	VI.—District Clerks	53
Article	VII.—Teachers	54
Article	VIII.—Schools	56
Article	IX.—Pupils	57
Article	X.—Duties of County Treasurer	58
Article	XI.—Duties of County Clerk, Clerk of District Court and Justices of the Peace	58
Article	XII.—Teachers' Institute	59
Article	XIII.—Examinations and Certificates	60
Article	XIV.—Compulsory attendance	64
Article	XV.—City Superintendent of Schools	66
Article	XVI.—School Funds	66
Article	XVII.—Bonds	71
Article	XVIII.—Vacancies	75
Article	XIX.—Tree Planting	76
Article	XX.—School Libraries	77
Article	XXI.—Miscellaneous	78

General School Law

OF THE

STATE OF MONTANA.

PROVISIONS OF THE ENABLING ACT.

Section 4. * * * And said (constitutional) conventions shall provide by ordinances irrevocable without the consent of the United States and the people of said states * * * * * * * *

Fourth. That provisions shall be made for the establishment and maintenance of systems of public schools, which shall be open to all children from said states, and free from sectarian control.

Section 10. That upon admission of each of said states into the Union, sections numbered 16 and 36 in every township of said proposed states, and where such sections or any parts thereof have been sold or otherwise disposed of by or under the authority of any act of Congress, other lands equivalent thereto, in legal subdivisions of not less than one quarter section, and as contiguous as may be to the section in lieu of which the same is taken, are hereby granted to said states for the support of common schools, such indemnity land to be selected within said states in such manner as the Legislature may provide, with the approval of the Secretary of the Interior; Provided: that the sixteenth and thirty-sixth sections embraced in permanent reservations for national purposes shall not, at any time, be subject to the grants nor to the idemnity provisions of this act, nor shall any lands embraced in Indian, military or other reservations of any character, be subject to the grants or to the indemnity provisions of this act until the reservation shall have been extinguished and such lands be restored to, and become a part of the public domain.

Section 11. That all lands herein granted for educational purposes shall be disposed of only at public sale, and at a price not less than ten (10) dollars per acre, the proceeds to constitute a permanent school fund, the interest of which only shall be expended in the support of said schools. But said lands may, under such regulation as the Legislature shall prescribe, be leased for periods of not more than five years, in quantities not exceeding one section to any one person or company; and such lands shall not be subject to pre-emption, homestead entry, or any other entry under the land laws of the United States, whether surveyed or unsurveyed, but shall be reserved for school purposes only.

Section 13. That 5 per centum of the proceeds of the sales of public lands lying within said states which shall be sold by the United States subsequent to the admission of said states into the Union, after deducting all the expenses incident to the same, shall be paid to the said states, to be used as a permanent fund, the interest of which only shall be expended for the support of common schools within said states respectively.

Section 14. That the lands granted to the Territories of Dakota and Montana by the act of February 18, 1881, entitled "An act to Grant Lands to Dakota, Montana, Arizona, Idaho and Wyoming, for University Purposes," are hereby vested in the states of South Dakota, North Dakota and Montana, respectively, if such states are admitted into the Union as provided in this act, to the extent of the full quantity of seventy-two sections to each of said states, and any portion of said lands that may not have been selected by either of said Territories of Dakota or Montana may be selected by the respective states aforesaid; but said act of February 18, 1881, shall be so amended as to provide that none of said lands shall be sold for less than ten (10) dollars per acre, and the proceeds shall constitute a permanent fund to be safely invested and held by said states severally, and the income thereof to be used exclusively for university purposes. * * * None of the lands granted in this section shall be sold at less than ten (10) dollars per acre; but said lands may be leased in the same manner as provided in Section 11 of this act. The schools, colleges, and universities provided for in this act shall forever remain under the exclusive control of said states, respectively, and no part of the proceeds arising from the sale or disposal of any lands herein granted for educational purposes shall be used for the support of any sectarian or denominational school, college or university. * * *

Section 16. That 90,000 acres of land to be selected and located as provided in Section 10 of this act, are hereby granted to each of said states except to the State of South Dakota, to which 120,000 acres are granted for the use and support of agricultural colleges in said states, as provided in the acts of Congress making donations of lands for such purposes.

Section 17. That in lieu of the grant of land for purposes of internal improvement made to new states by the eighth section of the act of September 4, 1841, which act is hereby repealed as to the states provided for by this act, and in lieu of any claim or demand by the said states, or either of them, under the act of September 28, 1850, and Section 2479 of the Revised Statutes, making a grant of swamp and overflowed lands to certain states, which grant it is hereby declared is not extended to the states provided for in this act, and in lieu of any grant of saline lands to said states, the following grants of land are hereby made, to-wit:

* * * To the State of Montana: For the establishment and maintenance of a School of Mines, 100,000 acres; for State Normal Schools, 100,000 acres; for Agricultural Colleges, in addition to the grant hereinbefore made for that purpose, 50,000 acres; for the establishment of a State Reform School, 50,000 acres; for the establishment of a Deaf and Dumb Asylum, 50,000 acres; for the public buildings at the Capital of the State, in addition to the grant hereinbefore made for that purpose, 150,000 acres.

* * * That the states provided for in this act shall not be entitled to any further or other grants of land for any purpose than as expressly provided for in this act. The lands granted by this section shall be held, appropriated and disposed of excusively for the purpose herein mentioned, in such manner as the Legislatures of the respective states may severally provide.

Section 18. That all mineral lands shall be exempted from the grants of this act. But if sections 16 and 36, or any subdivision or portion of any smallest subdivision thereof in any township shall be found by the Department of the Interior to be mineral lands, said states are hereby authorized and empowered to select, in legal subdivisions, an equal quantity of other unappropriated lands in said states, in lieu thereof, for the use and the benefit of the common schools of said states.

Section 19. That all lands granted in quantity or as indemnity by this act shall be selected, under the direction of the Secretary of the Interior, from the surveyed, unreserved and unappropriated public lands of the United States within the limits of the respective states entitled thereto. And there shall be deducted from the number of acres of land donated by this act for specific objects to said states the number of acres in each heretofore donated by Congress to said territories for similar objects.

CONSTITUTIONAL PROVISIONS.
(August 17th, 1889.)
PREAMBLE.

We, the people of Montana, grateful to Almighty God for the blessings of liberty, in order to secure the advantages of a State government, do, in accordance with the provisions of the Enabling Act of Congress, approved the 22nd of February, A. D. 1889, ordain and establish this Constitution.

ARTICLE V.
THE LEGISLATIVE DEPARTMENT.

Section 26. The Legislative Assembly shall not pass local or special laws in any of the following enumerated cases, that is to say:
* * * * * * * * * * * * * * * *

13. Providing for the management of common schools.

ARTICLE VII.
EXECUTIVE DEPARTMENT.

Section 1. The Executive department shall consist of a * * Superintendent of Public Instruction, each of whom shall hold his office for four years, or until his successor is elected and qualified, beginning on the first Monday of January next succeeding his election, except that the terms of office of those who are elected at the first election, shall begin when the State shall be admitted into the Union, and shall end on the first Monday of January, A. D. 1893. The officers of the Executive Department, excepting the Lieutenant Governor, shall during their terms of office reside at the seat of government where they shall keep the public records, books and papers. They shall perform such duties as are prescribed in this Constitution and by the laws of the State. * * * * * * * * * *

Section 3. No person shall be eligible to the office of * * * Superintendent of Public Instruction, unless he shall have attained the age of thirty years at the time of his election. * * * * In addition to the qualifications above prescribed, each of the officers named shall be a citizen of the United States, and have resided within the State or Territory two years next preceding his election.

Section 4. Until otherwise provided by law, the * * * Superintendent of Public Instruction, shall quarterly as due, during their continuance in office, receive for their services compensation which is fixed as follows: * * * * * * * *

Superintendent of Public Instruction, two thousand five hundred dollars per annum.

* * * The compensation enumerated shall be in full for all services by said officers respectively rendered in any official capacity or employment whatever during their respective terms of office, and the salary of no official shall be increased during his term of office. No officer named in this section shall receive, for the performance of any official duty, any fee for his own use, but all fees fixed by law for the performance by any officer of any official duty, shall be collected in advance, and deposited with the State Treasurer quarterly to the credit of the State. No officer mentioned in this section shall be eligible to, or hold any other public office, except member for the State Board of Education during his term of office.

ARTICLE IX.
ELECTIVE FRANCHISE.

Section 10. Women shall be eligible to hold the office of County Superintendent of schools or any school district office and shall have the right to vote at any school district election.

ARTICLE X.
STATE INSTITUTIONS.

Section 1. Educational, reformatory and penal institutions, and those for the benefit of the insane, blind, deaf and mute, soldiers' home, and such other institutions as the public good may require, shall be established and supported by the State in such a manner as may be prescribed by law.

ARTICLE XI.
EDUCATION.

Section 1. It shall be the duty of the Legislative Assembly of Montana to establish and maintain a general, uniform and thorough system of public, free common schools.

Section 2. The public school fund of the State shall consist of the proceeds of such lands as have heretofore been granted, or may hereafter be granted, to the State by the general government, known as school lands: and those granted in lieu of such lands acquired by gift or grant from any person or corporation under any law or grant of the general government; and of all other grants of land or money made to the State from the general government for general educational purposes, or where no other special purpose is indicated in such grant; all estates, or distributive shares of estates that may escheat to the State; all unclaimed shares and dividends of any corporation incorporated under the laws of the State, and all other grants, gifts, devises or bequests made to the State for general educational purposes.

Section 3. Such public school fund shall forever remain inviolate, guaranteed by the State against loss or diversion, to be invested, so far as possible, in public securities within the State, including school district bonds, issued for the erection of school buildings, under the restrictions to be provided by law.

Section 4. The Governor, Superintendent of Public Instruction, Secretary of State and Attorney General shall constitute the State Board of Land Commissioners, which shall have the direction, control, leasing and sale of the school lands of the State, and the lands granted or which may hereafter be granted for the support and benefit of the various State educational institutions, under such regulations and restrictions as may be prescribed by law.

Section 5. The interest on all invested school funds of the State, and all rents accruing from the leasing of any school lands, shall be apportioned to the several school districts of the State in proportion to the number of children and youths between the ages of six and twenty-one years, residing therein respectively, but no district shall be entitled to such distributive share that does not maintain a free public school for at least three months during the year for which distributions shall be made.

Section 6. It shall be the duty of the Legislative Assembly to provide by taxation, or otherwise, sufficient means, in connection with the amount received from the general school fund, to maintain a public, free, common school in each organized district in the State, for at least three months in each year.

Section 7. The public free schools of the State shall be open to all children and youth between the ages of six and twenty-one years.

Section 8. Neither the Legislative Assembly, nor any county, city, town, or school district, or other public corporations, shall ever make directly or indirectly, any appropriation, or pay from any public fund or moneys whatever, or make any grant of lands or other property in aid of any church, or for any sectarian purpose, or to aid in the support of any school, academy, seminary, college, university or other literary, scientific institution controlled in whole or in part by any church, sect or denomination whatever.

Section 9. No religious or partisan test or qualification shall ever be required of any person as a condition of admission into any public educational institution of the State, either as teacher or student; nor shall attendance be required at any religious service whatever, nor shall any sectarian tenets be taught in any public educational institution of the State; nor shall any person be debarred admission to any of the collegiate departments of the university on account of sex.

Section 10. The Legislative Assembly shall provide that all elections for school district officers shall be separate from those elections at which State or County officers are voted for.

Section 11. The general control and supervision of the State University and the various other State educational institutions shall be vested in a State Board of Education, whose powers and duties shall be prescribed and regulated by law. The said board shall consist of eleven members, the Governor, State Superintendent of Public Instruction and Attorney General, being ex-officio, the other eight members thereof, shall be appointed by the Governor subject to the confirmation of the Senate, under the regulation and restrictions to be provided by law.

Section 12. The funds of the State University and of all other State institutions of learning, from whatever source accruing, shall forever remain inviolate and sacred to the purpose for which they were dedicated. The various funds shall be respectively invested under such regulations as may be prescribed by law, and shall be guaranteed by the State against loss or diversion. The interest of said invested funds, together with the rents from leased lands or properties shall be devoted to the maintenance and perpetuation of these respective institutions.

ARTICLE XIII.
PUBLIC INDEBTEDNESS.

Section 6 No city, town, township or school district shall be allowed to become indebted in any manner or for any purpose to an amount, including existing indebtedness, in the aggregate exceeding three per centum of the value of the taxable property therein, to be ascertained by the last assessment for the State and County taxes previous to the incurring of such indebtedness, and all bonds or obligations in excess of such amount given by, or on behalf of, such city, town, township or school district shall be void; Provided, however, that the Legislative Assembly may extend the limit mentioned in this section, by authorizing municipal corporations to submit the question to a vote of the tax-payers affected thereby, when such increase is necessary to construct a sewerage system or to procure a supply of water for such municipality which shall own and control said water supply and devote the revenues derived therefrom to the payment of the debt.

ARTICLE XVII.
PUBLIC LANDS.

Section 1. All lands of the State that have been, or that may hereafter be granted to the State by Congress, and all lands acquired by gift or grant, or devise, from any person or corporation, shall be public lands of the State, and shall be held in trust for the people, to be disposed of as hereafter provided, for the respective purposes for which they have been or may be granted, donated or devised; and none of such land, nor any estate or interest therein, shall ever be disposed of except in pursuance of general laws providing for such disposition, nor unless the full market value of the estate or interest disposed of, to be ascertained in such manner as may be provided by law, be paid or safely secured to the State; nor shall any lands which the State holds by grant from the United States (in any case in which the manner of disposal and minimum price are so prescribed) be disposed of, except in the manner and for at least the price prescribed in the grant thereof, without the consent of the Untied States. Said lands shall be classified by the Board of Land Commissioners, as follows: First, lands which are valuable only for grazing purposes. Second, those which are principally valuable for the timber that is on them. Third, agricultural lands. Fourth, lands within the limits of any town or city or within three miles of such limits; Provided, That any of said lands may be re-classified whenever, by reason of increased facilities for irrigation or otherwise, they shall be subject to different classification.

Section 2. The lands of the first of said classes may be sold or leased, under such rules and regulations as may be prescribed by law. The lands of the second class may be sold, or the timber thereon may be sold, under such rules and regulations as may be prescribed by law. The agricultural lands may be either sold or leased, under such rules and regulations as may be prescribed by law. The land of the fourth class shall be sold in alternate lots of not more than five acres each, and not more than one-half of any one tract of such lands shall be sold prior to the year one thousand nine hundred and ten (1910).

Section 3. All public lands may be disposed of in such manner as may be provided by law.

STATUTORY PROVISIONS.

TITLE III.—EDUCATION.

Chapter.
- I. State Board of Education.
- II. State University of Montana.
- III. School of Mines of Montana.
- IV. Agricultural College of Montana.
- V. State Normal School.
- VI. Public Schools.
- VII. Deaf and Dumb Asylum.
- VIII. Authorizing State Board of Education to select lands for Educational Institutions.
- IX. Text-books.
- X. University Bond Act.
- XI. School of Mines Bond Act.
- XII. Deaf and Dumb Asylum Bond Act.
- XIII. Forms.

CHAPTER I.
STATE BOARD OF EDUCATION.

Section 1510. Membership.
Sec. 1511. Appointment and term.
Sec. 1512. Oath.
Sec. 1513. Officers.
Sec. 1514. Quorum.
Sec. 1515. Meetings.
Sec. 1516. Powers and duties.
Sec. 1517. State diplomas.
Sec. 1518. Life diplomas.
Sec. 1519. Graduate of the State Normal School.
Sec. 1520. Revocation of diploma.
Sec. 1521. Expenses.

Section 1510. The State Board of Education shall consist of eleven members, of which number the Governor, State Superintendent of Public Instruction and Attorney General shall be ex-officio members.

Section 1511. The Governor shall appoint by and with the advice and consent of the Senate the remaining eight members of the board. The persons first appointed under the provisions of this title shall hold office for the following terms: Two shall be appointed for the term of two years from the first day February, 1893; two for the term of three years from the first day of February, 1893; two for the term of four years from the first day of February, 1893, and two for the term of five years from the first day of February, 1893. Their successors shall be appointed for the term of four years, and until their successors are appointed and qualified.

Section 1512. The persons so appointed as members of the State Board of Education shall, before entering upon the duties of their office, take and subscribe the constitutional oath prescribed for civil officers, which shall be filed in the office of the Secretary of State.

Section 1513. The Governor shall be the President of the said Board and the Superintendent of Public Instruction shall be the Secretary thereof. The State Treasurer shall be the Treasurer of the Board.

Section 1514. A majority of said board shall constitute a quorum for the transaction of business.

Section 1515. The board shall hold semi-annual meetings at the State Capital on the first Monday in June and December in each year, and may hold special meetings at any time and place they may direct. The President and Secretary of the board may also call special meetings of said board at any time and place, if in their judgment the necessity requires it.

Section 1516. The powers and duties of said board shall be as follows:

First. They shall have the general control and supervision of the State University and the various State educational institutions.

Second. To adopt rules and regulations not inconsistent with the Constitution and laws of this State for its own government, and proper and necessary for the execution of the powers and duties conferred upon them by law.

Third. To prescribe rules and regulations for the government of the various State educational institutions.

Fourth. To recommend to the Legislature a uniform system of text books to be used in the public schools of the State below the high schools in accordance with the provisions of this Title.

Fifth. To grant diplomas to graduates of the State University and other State educational institutions, upon the recommendation of the faculties thereof, and may confer honorary degrees upon persons other than graduates, upon recommendation of the faculty of any of said institutions.

Sixth. To adopt and use in the authentication of its acts an official seal.

Seventh. To grant State diplomas, valid for six years, and life diplomas.

Eighth. To keep a record of its proceedings.

Ninth. To make an annual report on or before the first day of January, which shall be printed under the direction of the board.

Tenth. To receive from the State Board of Land Commissioners or other boards or persons ,or from the government of the United States, any and all funds, income and other property, to which any of the said institutions may be entitled, and to use and appropriate the same for the specific purpose of the grant or donation, and none other and to have general control of all receipts and disbursements of any of said institutions.

Eleventh. To appoint and commission experienced teachers to act as instructors in county institutes.

Section 1517. State diplomas shall be issued to such persons as have a good moral character and who have held for one year and still hold in full force and effect a first grade county certificate, with the addition of English literature and mental philosophy and who shall furnish satisfactory evidence of having been successfully engaged in teaching for at least five years. The term "five years" shall be construed to mean for five years of not less than seven months each; that is, the applicant must have taught a part of each year for five years—not necessarily consecutive years—and in all thirty-five months, of which at least twenty-one months must have been in the public schools of Montana; provided, that the StateBoard of Education shall have power to add such other studies to those enumerated in this section as they may deem necessary.

Section 1518. Life diplomas may be issued upon all the same conditions as State diplomas, except that the applicant must pass a satisfactory examination upon the rudiments of botany, geology, political economy, zoology and general history, and must furnish satisfactory evidence of having been successfully engaged in teaching for at least ten years. "Ten years" shall be construed to mean ten years of not less than seven months each; that is, the applicant must have taught some part of each year for ten years—not necessarily consecutive years —and in all seventy months, of which at least twenty-one months must have been in the public schools of Montana.

Section 1519. A State or life diploma may be granted to any graduate of the State Normal School of Montana or of the State University of Montana, when the said graduate furnishes satisfactory evidence of having successfully taught, after graduation, a public school in this State for sixteen school months. State or life diplomas may be granted to graduates of other educational institutions, within or without the State, upon conditions established by the State Board of Education.

Section 1520. Any State or life diploma may be revoked by the State Superintendent for incompetency or immoral conduct, but before any such revocation, the holder shall be served with a written statement of the charges against him, and shall have an opportunity for defense before said State Board of Education.

Section 1521. The members of said board shall receive no compensation for their services, but shall be allowed their actual traveling expenses incurred in attending the meetings of the board, which expenses and all other expnses on the certificate of the Secretary of the board, shall be audited and approved by the State Board of Examiners, and paid by warrant of the State Auditor on the State Treasurer.

CHAPTER II.
UNIVERSITY OF MONTANA.

Section 1543. The University of Montana established.
Sec. 1544. Government. Officers.
Sec. 1545. Duty of State Board of Education.
Sec. 1546. Power of State Board of Education.
Sec. 1547. Officers of University. Report.
Sec. 1548. Objects of University.
Sec. 1549. Course of study.
Sec. 1550. Qualifications of students. Military instructions.
Sec. 1551. Charges for tuition.
Sec. 1552. Endowed professorships.
Sec. 1553. Appropriations for support of University.
Sec. 1554. Selection of site.

Section 1543. There is hereby established in this State at the City of Missoula an institution of learning under the name and style of "The University of Montana."

Section 1544. The government of the University shall be vested in the State Board of Education. The manner of their appointment, their powers, duties, compensation and terms of office shall be as prescribed by law. The State Treasurer shall be the Treasurer of said Board, and perform all the duties of such office, subject to such regulations as the State Board of Education may adopt, not inconsistent with his official duties; and he and his sureties shall be liable on his official bond as State Treasurer for the faithful discharge of such duties.

Section 1545. The State Board of Education shall have power, and it shall be their duty, to enact by-laws for the government of the

University in all its departments; to elect a President of the University, and in their discretion a Vice-President, and the requisite number of Professors, instructors, officers and employes, and fix their salaries and terms of each; to determine the moral and educational qualifications of applicants for admission to the various courses of instruction; but no sectarian or partisan test shall ever be allowed or exercised in the appointment of professors, instructors, officers or employes of the University, or in the admission of students thereto, or for any purpose whatever. No instruction, either sectarian or religious or partisan in politics, shall ever be allowed in any department in the University. The State Board of Education shall have power to regulate the course of instruction and prescribe the text books and authorities to be used in all the departments, and may confer such degrees, and grant such diplomas as are usual in Universities; and may confer the usual honorary degrees upon other persons than graduates of the University in recognition of their learning, or devotion to literature, art or science, as may be recommended by the Faculty of the University.

Section 1546. The immediate government of the several colleges of the University shall be intrusted to their respective Faculties; but the State Board of Education shall have the control of all books, records, buildings, grounds and all other property of the University.

Section 1547. The President of the University shall be the President of the General Faculty, and of the special Faculties of the several departments or colleges and the Executive head of the institution in all its departments. As such officer he shall have authority, subject to the State Board of Education, to give general direction to the instruction, practical affairs and scientific investigations of the several colleges, and as long as the interest of the institution require it, he shall be charged with the duties of one of the Professorships. He shall perform the duties of a Corresponding Secretary for the University. He shall, annually, on or before the fifteenth day of December in each year, make a report to the State Board of Education, showing in detail the progress and condition of the University during the previous year, the number of Professors and students in the several departments and classes, the nature and results of all important experiments and investigations, and such other matters, relating to the proper government and educational work of the institution as he shall deem useful.

Section 1548. The object of the University of Montana shall be to provide the best and most efficient manner of imparting to young men and women, on equal terms, a liberal education and thorough knowledge of the different branches of literature, science and the arts, with the varied applications, and to this end there shall be established the following colleges or departments, to-wit:

First. A preparatory department.

Second. A department of literature, science and the arts.

Third. Such professional and technical colleges as may, from time time to time, be added thereto or connected therewith. The preparatory department may be dispensed with, at such rate and in such wise as may seem just and proper to the State Board of Education.

Section 1549. Such duties or courses of instruction shall be pursued in the preparatory department as shall best prepare the student to enter any of the regular colleges or departments of the University. The college or department of Literature, Science and the Arts shall embrace courses of instruction in mathematical, physical and natural sciences, with their application to the industrial arts; a liberal course of instruction in the languages, literature, history and philosophy, and such other branches as the State Board of Education may prescribe.

And, as soon as the income of the University will allow, and in such order as the demands of the public seem to require, the said courses of instruction in the sciences, literature and the arts shall be expanded into distinct colleges or departments of the University, each with its own Faculty and appropriate title.

Section 1550. The University shall be open to students of both sexes, under such regulations and restrictions as the State Board of Education may deem proper. All able-bodied male students of the University may receive instruction and discipline in military tactics, the requisite arms of which shall be furnished by the State.

Section 1551. Tuition shal ever be free to all students who shall have been residents of the State for one year next preceding their admission, except in the law and Medical Departments and for extra studies. The State Board of Education may prescribe rates for tuition for any student in the Law and Medical departments, or who shall not have been a resident as aforesaid, and for teaching such studies.

Section 1552. Any person contributing a sum not less than fifteen thousand dollars shall have the privilege of endowing a Professorship in the University, or any department thereof, the name and object of which shall be designated by the State Board of Education.

Section 1553. For the support and endowment of the University there is annually and perpetually appropriated:

First. The University Income Fund, and all other sums of money appropriated by law to the University Income Fund.

Second. All tuition and matriculation fees.

Third. All such contributions as may be derived from public or private bounty.

The entire income of all such funds shall be placed at the disposal of the State Board of Education, by transfer to the Treasurer of said Board, and to be kept separate and distinct from the accounts of the State, and all other funds, and to be used solely for the support of the aforesaid colleges and departments of the University or connection therewith. But all means derived from other public or private bounty shall be exclusively devoted to the specific objects for which they shall have been designated by the donor.

Section 1554. It shall be the duty of the State Board of Education within ninety (90) days from the date of the passage of this act, if then organized, but if not organized then within ninety (90) days from the organization of the said Board, to select the site for the definite and permanent location of said University of Montana, which site shall be within three miles of the city limits of the City of Missoula; and they shall, at once, take steps or proceedings for procuring the title to the tract or tracts of land so selected by them, and they may, and are hereby empowered to enter into contracts, in the name of the State of Montana, for the purchase of said tract or tracts of land so selected, and may execute such obligations for the payment of the same as will mature when the probable income of the University fund will pay for the same. The State Board of Education are hereby authorized and empowered to accept, in the name of the State of Montana, such gifts of land and moneys as may be tendered for a University site or to aid in the purchase of said site; and they shall take the proper and necessary conveyances of said tract or tracts of land in the name of the State. Provided, That if such gifts consist of money only or money and land, and the land be not sufficient in amount or not appropriate for a University site, then they shall appropriate such gifts to the payment of said site, and if there be a surplus the same to become a part of the University fund. Provided, that said tract of land shall not be less than forty (40) acres in extent.

CHAPTER III.
SCHOOL OF MINES.

Section 1572. Schol of Mines established.
Sec. 1573. Trustees, term, quorum.
Sec. 1574. Appointment of trustees.
Sec. 1575. Oath.
Sec. 1576. Powers of trustees.
Sec. 1577. Object of school.
Sec. 1578. Site, appliances.
Sec. 1579. Qualifications of students.
Sec. 1580. Officers of Board.
Sec. 1581. Vacancies in Board, how filled.
Sec. 1582. Report.
Sec. 1583. Location of school lands.
Sec. 1584. Revenue of school.
Sec. 1585. Investment of donations.
Sec. 1586. Bond of Treasurer.
Sec. 1587. Fees of Professors.
Sec. 1588. Debt prohibited.
Sec. 1589. Faculy of School.
Sec. 1590. Trustees may accept donations.

Section 1572. The State School of Mines is hereby established and declared to be a body corporate under the name of "Montana State School of Mines" and by that name may sue and be sued, may take and hold real or personal property by gift, bequest, devise, or purchase from the State, and may dispose of the same when authorized so to do by law.

Section 1573. There shall be a Board of Trustees of said School of Mines, to be composed of five persons, who shall, except as hereinafter provided, hold their office for a period of four years and until their successors are appointed and qualified. Any three of said Board of Trustees shall constitute a quorum for the transaction of business and the said Board shall have such powers and perform such duties as are hereinafter specified.

Section 1574. The State Board of Education shall within ninety (90) days of the passage of this Act, if such Board shall then be organized, and if not so organized, shall within ninety (90) days after their organization designate and apppoint five suitable persons, at least three of whom shall be residents of Silver Bow County; and the persons so appointed by the State Board of Education shall be known as the Trustees of the School of Mines, three of whom shall hold office until Jnauary 1st, 1896, and two of whom shall hold office until January 1st, 1894, and their terms of office shall be distinctly designated by the State Board of Education.

Section 1575. Every Trustee hereafter appointed shall, before entering upon the duties of his office, take an oath to support the Constitution of the United States and the Constitution of the State of Montana, and to faithfully perform the duties of his said office of Trustee to the best of his ability and undersanding.

Section 1576. The said Board of Trustees shall have the control and management of the said School of Mines, and of the property belonging thereto, subject to the laws of this State, and to such general control and supervision as shall be vested by law in the State Board of Education, and may make all needful by-laws and regulations for the government of said Board, and for the management and government of said School of Mines not inconsistent with the laws of this State.

Section 1577. It shall be the object of such School of Mines to furnish facilities for the education of such persons as may desire to receive special instruction in Chemistry, Metallurgy, Mineralogy, Geology, Mining, Mining Engineering, Mathematics, Mechanics and Drawing.

Section 1578. The said Board of Trustees are hereby authorized to procure a suitable site at or near the City of Butte, in the County of Silver Bow, and the State of Montana, for said School of Mines, as hereinafter set out, and to erect suitable buildings thereon, and to procure such machinery and other appliances as may be necessary to carry out the object and intention of such institution and to promote the welfare thereof, whenever the funds provided for the establishment of said School of Mines will warrant the same.

Section 1579. The said School of Mines shall be open and free for instruction to all bona fide residents of this State without regard to sex or color, and, with the consent of said Board students from other States or Territories may receive an education thereat, upon such terms and at such rates of tuition as the Board may prescribe.

Section 1580. The Board shall, at their first meeting, and bi-ennially thereafter, elect one of their number Chairman of said Board, and shall also appoint a Secretary and Treasurer, either from their own number, or other suitable persons, as they may deem best, and prescribe their duties, and may at any time, in their discretion, remove such Secretary or Treasurer.

Section 1581. The State Board of Education, with the advice and consent of the Senate shall, at each regular sesssion of the Legislative Assembly, to be held after the year A. D. 1893, by appointment fill the vacancies in said Board of Trustees, occurring either by the expiration of their term of office or otherwise; and any vacancy occurring in such Board of Trustees, when the Legislative Assembly is not in session, may be temporarily filled by the State Board of Education, until the next meeting of the Legislative Assembly.

Section 1582. The Chairman of the Board of Trustees shall annually, on or before the 10th day of December in each year, make a report to the State Board of Education of the prosperity and condition of said School of Mines, containing such statistical and other information pertaining thereto as he may deem necessary and useful, and also a detailed statement of the receipts and expenses of such institution.

Section 1583. The State Board of Land Commissioners are hereby authorized and required to locate all the lands that have been donated by the United States to the State of Montana for the establishment and maintenance of a School of Mines, and report to the next Legislative Assembly the number of acres so located, where situated, their character and estimated value, and shall make a similar report on or before the next meeting of the Legislative Assembly to the Board of Trustees of the School of Mines, and also to the State Board of Education.

Section 1584. None of the land located, as required in the preceding section of this Act, shall be sold, except as may be provided by the Legislative Assembly, and whenever the said lands are sold the proceeds of such sale, being for the whole or a part of said lands, shall be paid over to the said Board of Trustees by an order drawn by the President of the School of Mines, countersigned by the Secretary of the Board, the President and Secretary having been so authorized by the Board of Trustees, upon the State Treasurer. All revenue and profits arising from the said lands shall be paid over to the Board of Trustees in like manner. The said Board of Trustees, with the advice and consent of the State Board of Education, shall set apart a certain proportion of the said money whether derived from the sale of said lands or the revenues and profits of said lands, for a building fund, which proportion shall be by the said Board of Trustees used in procuring a suitable site for said School of Mines, and the erection of such buildings and the procuring of such machinery and other appliances as may be necessary to carry out the object and intention of such institution. The residue of said money so paid and arising from the sale of said lands shall be forever kept as a fund for the said School of Mines, no part of the principal of which shall ever be expended for any purpose whatever, but the income of said fund may be used under the direction of the Board of Trustees for the general purposes of the school. No funds of the School of Mines shall ever be directly or indirectly loaned to the Chairman or any of the Trustees, Professors or other officers of the school. The permanent funds of the school shall be invested by the Board of Trustees, first in bonds of the State of Montana if such are to be had, but if not, then in bonds of the United States, and said funds shal not be invested in any other manner or upon any other securities whatever.

Section 1585. All donations of money, scurities or other property, shall be conveyed to the Board of Trustees of the school and invested as other funds of the school.

Section 1586. The said Board of Trustees shall require the Treasurer of the School of Mines to give such bonds as they may deem sufficient to protect said institution against loss of any funds which may come into his hands as such Treasurer, conditioned for the safe keeping and faithful disbursement thereof, and the said Treasurer of the School of Mines shall not pay out any of the funds which shall come into his hands as such Treasurer, except under the order of the Chairman of the School of Mines, countersigned by the Secretary thereof.

Section 1587. It shall be lawful for the Professor or President of the School of Mines, who shall be appointed by the said Board of Trustees, to charge and collect such reasonable fees for any and all assays and analyses made by them, as the said Board may prescribe, an account of which shall be kept by said President and paid over monthly to the Treasurer of said School of Mines, which shall become a part of the School of Mines fund.

Section 1588. The Board of Trustees are hereby prohibited from creating any debt as against the School of Mines, buildings, machinery or appliances, or in any manner incumbering the same, or of incurring any expense beyond their ability to pay from the annual income of the School of Mines for the current year.

Section 1589. The Board of Trustees are empowered to select a President and Faculty, and such Professors and teachers as may be necessary to properly conduct the said School of Mines, and the President so selected shall be the President of the Faculty and Board of and disposed of as other property or funds provided for said School. Teachers employed for said school.

Section 1590. The Board of Trustees are authorized to accept any donations of land, money or other property offered for the use and benefit of said School of Mines, and to take proper deeds or conveyances of the same in their own name for the sole and exclusive use of said school, such donations, gifts or bequests to be invested, used

CHAPTER IV.

AGRICULTURAL COLLEGE OF MONTANA.

Section 1622. Establishment and location.
Sec. 1623. Selection of site.
Sec. 1624. Control of College.
Sec. 1625. Executive Board.
Sec. 1626. Officers of College.
Sec. 1627. Secretary and Treasurer of Board.
Sec. 1628. Agricultural Experiment Station.
Sec. 1629. Management of Station.

Section 1622. The Agricultural College of the State of Montana is established and located at the City of Bozeman, or within three (3) miles of the corporate limits of said City, upon such tract, or tracts of land, conforming in the aggregate not less than eighty (80) acres, and as much more as shall be selected by the State Board of Education as hereinafter provided; and said College has for its leading objects and purposes, without excluding other scientific and classical studies, and including military tactics, to teach such branches of learning as are related to agriculture and the mechanic arts, in such manner as the State Board of Education, and any subordinate Boards by such State Board appointed, may prescribe.

Section 1623. It shall be the duty of the State Board of Education, within ninety (90) days from the date of the passage of this Act, if then organized, but if not organized then within ninety (90) days from the organization of the said Board, to select the site for the definite and permanent location of said Agricultural College of Montana and Agricultural Experiment Station, which site shall be at the City of Bozeman, or within three (3) miles of the corporate limits of said City of Bozeman; and said State Board of Education shall at once take steps or proceedings for procuring the title to the tract or tracts of land so selected by them and they may and are hereby empowered to enter into contracts in the name of the State of Montana, for the purchase of said tract or tracts of land so selected, and may execute such obligations for the payment of the same as will mature when the probable income from the fund of said Agricultural College and Agricultural Experiment Station, or either of them, will pay for the same. The said Board of Education are hereby authorized and empowered to accept in the name of the State of Montana such gifts of land and money as may be tendered to aid in the purchase of said site, and whenever such gifts are sufficient in amount to secure or pay for said site they shall appropriate the same to that purpose, and take the proper and necessary conveyances of said tract or tracts of land in the name of the State. All lands and money acquired, as provided in this section, shall be taken and held for the sole use and benefit of said Agricultural College and said Agricultural Experiment Station.

Section 1624. The general control and supervision of such College is vested in the State Board of Education, which Board may prescribe all rules therefor.

Section 1625. The Governor, by and with the advice and consent of the State Board of Education, may designate and appoint an Executive Board, consisting of five (5) members, at least three (3) of whom shall be residents of the County wherein said institution is situated, which Executive Board shall have the immediate direction and control of the affairs of said College, subject only to the general supervision and control of said State Board of Education. Such Executive Board shall serve during the term of the State Board of Education, unless sooner removed.

Section 1626. The Executive Board is authorized to choose and appoint a President and Faculty of said College, who shall serve as such, for such time, and receive such compensation as the said Executive Board may prescribe, subject to the approval of the State Board of Education.

Section 1627. The Executive Board shall appoint a Secretary thereof, who may also act as Treasurer of said Board and who may not be a member thereof, and such Secretary and Treasurer shall give bond with good and sufficient surety for the faithful performance of his duties as such, and for the faithful accounting for any paying over to the said State Board of Education, to and for the use of said College, all moneys received by him as Treasurer, in such sum as said State Board of Education may prescribe.

Section 1628. There is also located and established on the lands so to be selected by the State Board of Education, in connection with said Agricultural College and under its direction, an Agricultural Experiment Station, to aid in acquiring and diffusing among the people of the State of Montana useful and practical information on subjects connected with Agriculture, and to promote scientific investigation and experiments respecting the principles and application of agricultural science, which Experiment Station is established under and by virtue of the authority contained in the Act of Congress entitled "An Act to establish Experimental Stations in connection with the Colleges established in the several States, under provisions of an Act approved July 2d, 1862, and the said Acts supplementary thereto," approved March 2d, 1887, and the provisions, donations and benefits contained in said Act of Congress, and in all other Acts of Congress relating to Agricultural Experiment Stations and Agricultural Colleges, now in force, and all Acts supplementary thereto, or amendatory thereof, are by the State of Montana hereby accepted and adopted.

Section 1629. Said Agricultural Experiment Station is hereby placed under the supervision and control of the State Board of Education, and the Executive or subordinate Board or authority who may be by the Governor, by and with the consent and advice of said State Board of Education, appointed.

CHAPTER V.
STATE NORMAL SCHOOL.

Section 1652. Established and located.
Sec. 1653. Object of School.
Sec. 1654. Control and Supervision.
Sec. 1655. Acceptance of public lands.
Sec. 1656. Committee of Buildings.
Sections 1657 and 1658 Act approved February 22, 1899.)

Section 1652. That there be and hereby is established a State Normal School within two miles of the corporate limits of the City of Dillon, Beaverhead County, Montana, which shall be callled "The State Normal School at Dillon."

Section 1653. The object of said Normal School shall be the instruction and training of teachers for the public schools of the State.

Section 1654. The control and supervision of such school is vested in the State Board of Education, which must elect a President, all teachers and employes, and prescribe all necessary rules therefor.

Section 1655. The State Board of Education, herein mentioned, and their successors, shall receive, in the name of the State Normal School hereby established, all the benefits, of whatsoever nature, that may be derived from the distribution and selection of lands contemplated in Section 17, of an Act of Congress, approved February 22nd, 1889, entitled "An Act to provide for the division of Dakota into two States, and to enable the people of North Dakota, South Dakota, Montana and Washington to form constitutions and State governments, and to be admitted into the Union on an equal footing with the original State and to make donations of public lands to such States."

Section 1656. The Governor, by and with the advice and consent of the State Board of Education, may designate and appoint an executive board, consisting of five members, at least three of whom shall be residents of the county wherein the said institution is siutated, which executive board shall have the immediate direction and control of the affairs of said school, subject only to the general supervision of

the State Board of Education, and such executive board shall serve during the term of the State Board of Education, unless sooner removed by the Governor. The Executive Board is authorized to choose and appoint a President and faculty of said School, who shall serve as such for such time and receive such compensation as the executive board may prescribe, subject however at all times to the approval of the State Board of Education. The Executive Board shall appoint a secretary thereof, who may also act as treasurer of the said board, and who may not be a member thereof, and such secretary and treasurer shall give a bond with good and sufficient surety for the faithful performance of his duties as such, and for the faithful accounting for and paying over to the State Board of Education, to and for the use of said school, all moneys received by him as treasurer, in such sum as said State Board of Education may prescribe. The said State Board of Education is hereby authorized and empowered to accept for and on account of, and for the use and benefit of the said Normal School, any bequests and donations to the State, made for the use and benefit of said school.
(Sec. 1656 Act approved March 4, 1897.)

Section 1657. All graduates of the State Normal School who have completed and graduated in the professional course of the three year's course of said school and received a diploma, certifying that either of the said courses, has been completed, shall, on the registry of said diploma in the office of the State Superintendent of Public Instruction, be entitled to teach in the public schools of the State of Montana without other or further examination, for the term of three years after such graduation and such graduates shall, on furnishing to the State Board of Education satisfactory evidence of having successfully taught in the public schools of the State for a term of two years, be entitled to receive from said Board a life diploma.

Section 1658. All graduates of the said State Normal School who have completed and graduated in the four years course of said school and received a diploma, certifying that said course has been completed, shall, on the registry of said diploma in the office of the State Superintendent of Public Instruction, be entitled to teach in the public schools of the State of Montana, without other or further examination, for a term of three years after such graduation, and on furnishing to the State Board of Education satisfactory evidence of having successfully taught in the public schools of Montana for a period of one year, shall be entitled to receive from such Board a life diploma.

CHAPTER VI.
PUBLIC SCHOOLS.

Article.
- I. Superintendent of Public Instruction.
- II. County Superintendent of Schools.
- III. School Districts.
- IV. Election of School Trustees.
- V. Board of Trustees.
- VI. District Clerks.
- VII. Teachers.
- VIII. Schools.
- IX. Pupils.
- X. Duties of the County Treasurer.
- XI. Duties of the County Clerk, Clerk of the District Court and the Justices of the Peace.
- XII. Teachers' Institutes.
- XIII. Examinations and Certificates.
- XIV. Compulsory Attendance.
- XV. City Superintendent of Schools.
- XVI. School Funds.
- XVII. Bonds.
- XVIII. Vacancies.
- XIX. Tree Planting.
- XX. School Libraries.
- XXI. Miscellaneous.

ARTICLE I.
STATE SUPERINTENDENT OF PUBLIC INSTRUCTION.

Sec.
- 1700. Election, qualification, oath and bond.
- 1701. Duties.
- 1702. General powers.
- 1703. Duty. Blanks.
- 1704. Same. Examinations.
- 1705. Same. Course of study.
- 1706. Same. Institute rules.
- 1707. Same. County Superintendents.
- 1708. Same. Records.

Sec.
- 1709. Same. School laws.
- 1710. Same. Seal.
- 1711. Same. Institutes.
- 1712. Same. Report.
- 1713. Same.
- 1714. Apportionment of school fund.
- 1715. Clerk. Salary.
- 1716. Superintendent's Salary.
- 1717. Expenses.

Section 1700. There shall be chosen by the qualified electors of the State at the time and place of voting for members of the Legislature, a Superintendent of Public Instruction, who shall have attained the age of thirty years at the time of his election and shall have resided within the State two years next preceding his election, and is the holder of a State certificate of the highest grade, issued in some State, or is a graduate of some reputable university, college or normal school. He shall hold his office at the seat of government for the term of four years from the first Monday in January following his election, and until his successor is elected and qualified. Before entering upon his duties he shall take the oath of civil officers and give a bond, in the penal sum of ten thousand dollars, with not less than two sureties, to be approved by the Governor and Attorney General.

Section 1701. The Superintendent shall preserve in his office all books, maps, charts, works on education, school reports and school laws of other States and cities, plans for school buildings, and other articles of educational interest and value, which may come into his possession as such officer, and, at the expiration of his term, shall deliver them, together with the reports, statements, records and archives of his office to his successor.

Section 1702. He shall have the general supervision of the public schools of the State.

Section 1703. He shall prepare, cause to be printed and furnish to the proper officers or persons all school registers, reports, statements, notices and blanks for returns needed or required to be used in the schools or by the school officers in the State. He shall prepare and furnish to school officers, through the County Superintendents, lists of publications approved by him as suitable for school libraries; such lists shall contain also the lowest price at which each publication can be purchased and the terms. He shall also prescribe rules and instructions for the proper care and use of school libraries and such other information relative thereto as he shall think needful.

Section 1704. He shall prepare all questions to be used in the examination of applicants for teachers' county certificates, and prescribe the rules and regulations for conducting all such examinations.

Section 1705. He shall prepare and prescribe a course of study for all the public schools of the State.

Section 1706. He shall prescribe rules and regulations for the holding of teachers' institutes.

Section 1707. He shall counsel with and advise County Superintendents upon all matters involving the welfare of the schools; he shall, when requested, give them written answers to all questions concerning the school law. He shall decide all appeals from the decision of the County Superintendents, and may for such decision require affidavits, verified statements or sworn testimony as to the facts in issue. He shall prescribe and cause to be enforced ruls of practice and regulations pertaining to the hearing and determining of appeals and necessary for carrying into effect the school laws of the State.

Section 1708. He shall keep a record of his official acts and shall file in his office all appeals and papers pertaining thereto.

Section 1709. He shall at least once in four years cause to be printed the school laws of the State, with such notes and decisions thereon as may seem to him advisable, and shall furnish them as they are needed to the school officers in the State.

Section 1710. He shall provide and keep a seal, which shall be the official seal of the State Superintendent of Public Instruction and by which all of his official acts may be authenticated.

Section 1711. He shall attend and assist at teachers institutes and aid, and encourage generally, teachers in qualifying themselves for the successful discharge of their duties. He shall also as far as he shall find practicable address public assemblies on subjects pertaining to public schools, and shall labor faithfully in all practicable ways for the welfare of the public schools of the State and shall perform such other duties as shall be required of him by the law.

Section 1712. He shall, on or before the first day of December preceding the bi-ennial session of the Legislative Assembly, make and transmit to the Governor a report, showing:

First. The number of districts; schools, teachers employed and pupils taught therein, and the attendance of pupils and studies pursued by them.

Second. The financial condition of the schools, their receipts and expenditures, value of school houses and property, cost of tuition and wages of teachers.

Third. The condition, educational and financial, of the Normal and higher institutions connected with the school system of the State, and, as far as it can be ascertained, of the private schools, academies and colleges of the State.

Fourth. Such general matters, information and recommendations relating to the educational interests of the State as he may deem important.

Section 1713. Fifteen hundred copies of the report of the Superintendent of Public Instruction shall be printed biennially in the month of December preceding the session of the Legislative Assembly. Two copies shall be furnished to each of the members of the Legislative Assembly, one copy to each County Superintendent of the State, one copy to the clerk of each school board, two to each State officer, one to each State and Territorial Superintendent; fifty copies shall be filed in the office of the Superintendent of Public Instruction and ten in the State Historical Library. The balance shall be distributed among the various colleges, university and other libraries of the United States.

Section 1714. He shall, between the first and tenth days of February of each year, apportion the State School Fund among the several counties of the State in proportion to the number of children of school age in each, as shown by the last enumeration authorized by law. It shall be the duty of the State Board of Land Commissioners to notify the StateAuditor on or before the tenth day of January of each year the amount of the State School Fund subject to apportionment; and the said Auditor immediately upon receipt of such notification shall issue his warrant on the State Treasurer for the said amount. Thereupon the State Treasurer shall certify said apportionment to the several county treasurers not later than the first Monday in March; Provided, That the several county treasurers have fully complied with Section 183 of "An Act Concerning Revenue," approved March 6th, 1891; in which case the county treasurers, upon receiving notice from the State Treasurer of the amounts due their counties from the State School Fund, may deduct said amount from the amount found due the State by their counties and remit the balance to the State Treasurer. The Superintendent of Public Instruction shall certify to the county superintendent of schools of each county the amount apportioned to that county.

Section 1715. The Superintendent of Public Instruction shall have power to appoint one clerk, who shall receive an annal salary of fifteen hundred dollars, and shall perform such duties pertaining to the office as the Superintendent may direct. Said clerk shall also perform the duties of the clerk of the State Board of Education.

Section 1716. The Superintendent shall receive an annual salary of twenty-five hundred dollars to be paid quarterly on the warrant of the State Auditor. He shall also be paid his traveling expenses necessarily incurred in the discharge of his duties, not to exceed five hundred dollars in any one year.

Section 1717. All necessary expenditures of money incurred by the Superintendent of Public Instruction for postage, stationery, printing and expressage, not exceeding two hundred and fifty dollars in any one year, shall be paid by the State.

ARTICLE II.

COUNTY SUPERINTENDENT OF SCHOOLS.

Sec.		Sec.	
1730.	Election, Term, Oath, Bond.	1738.	Presides at Institutes.
1731.	General Powers.	1739.	May issue temporary certificates.
1732.	Duty, Visiting Schools.	1740.	Annual report.
1733.	Same. Blanks.	1741.	Boundaries of School District.
1734.	Same. Record.	1742.	Office, Stationery.
1735.	Same. Controversies.	1743.	Must not teach.
1736.	Same. May administer oaths.	1744.	Qualifications.
1737.	Shall apportion school moneys.		

Section 1730. A county superintendent of schools shall be elected in each organized county in this State at the general election preceding the expiration of the term of office of the present incumbent, and every two years thereafter, who shall take office on the first Monday in January next succeeding his election, and hold for two years, or until his successor is elected and qualified. The person so elected shall take the oath or affirmation of office, and shall give an official bond to the county in a sum to be fixed by the board of county commissioners of said county. The county commissioners of any county shall by appointment, fill any vacancy that may occur in the office of county superintendent until the next general election: Provided, that all persons otherwise qualified shall be eligible to the said office of county superintendent of common schools without regard to sex.

Section 1731. The county superintendent shall have the general supervision of the public schools in his county.

Section 1732. He shall visit every public school under his supervision at least once each official year, and oftener if he shall deem it necessary to increase its usefulness. He shall at such visit carefully observe the condition of the school, the mental and moral instruction given, the methods employed by the teacher in teaching, training and drill; the teacher's ability and progress of the pupils. He shall advise and direct the teacher in regard to the instruction, classification, government and discipline of the school and the course of study. He shall keep a record of such visits and by memoranda indicate his judgment of the teacher's ability to teach and govern, and the condition and progress of the school, which shall be open to inspection to any school trustee.

Section 1733. He shall carry into effect all instructions of the State Superintendent, given within his authority. He shall distribute to the proper officers and to teachers all blanks furnished him by the State Superintendent and needed by such officer and teachers.

Section 1734. He shall keep a record of all his official acts. He shall preserve all books, maps, charts and apparatus sent him as a school officer, or belonging to his office. He shall file all reports and statements from teachers and school boards and shall turn them over to his successor in office.

Section 1735. He shall decide all matters in controversy arising in his county in the administration of the school law or appealed to him from the decisions of school officers or boards. An appeal may be taken from his decision, in which case a full written statement of the facts, together with the testimony and his decision in the case, shall be certified to the State Superintendent for his decision in the matter, which decision shall be final, subject to adjudication or the proper legal remedies in the State courts.

Section 1736. The county superintendent shall have power to administer oaths of office to all subordinate school officers, and to witnesses, and to examine them under oath in case of appeal, of petition, of revoking the certificate of a teacher, and in all controversies and questions arising in the administration of the school laws brought or coming before him for opinion, order or decision; but he shall not receive pay for administering such oaths.

Section 1737. The county superintendent shall apportion all school moneys to the school districts in accordance with the provisions of this title quarterly, and he may make apportionments at such other times as may be required or deemed necessary for the convenience of school officers. He shall certify to the several district clerks and county treasurers the amount so apportioned to the several districts, and the trustees shall draw their warrants on the county treasurer in favor of persons entitled to receive the same. Such warrant shall show for what purpose the money is required, and no such warrant shall be drawn unless there is money in the treasury to the credit of such district.

Section 1738. He shall preside over all teachers' institutes held in his county, and shall elect suitable persons to instruct therein from the list of teachers commissioned by the State Board of Education.

Section 1739. He shall have power to issue, if he deem it proper to do so, temporary certificates, valid until the next regular examination to persons holding certificates of like grade granted in other counties, or upon any certificates or diplomas possessed by the applicant showing his fitness for the profession of teaching: Provided, that no person shall be entitled to receive such temporary certificate more than once in the same county.

Section 1740. He shall, on or before the first day of November each year, make and transmit an annual report to the Superintendent of Public Instruction, containing such statistics, items and statements, relative to the schools of the county, as may be required and prescribed by the Superintendent of Public Instruction. Such reports shall be made upon and conform to the blanks furnished by the Superintendent of Public Instruction for that purpose. He shall not be paid his salary for the last month in his official year until he presents to the county commissioners the receipt of the Superintendent of Public Instruction for such annual report.

Section 1741. The county superintendent shall inquire and ascertain whether the boundaries of school districts in his county are definitely and plainly described in the records of the board of county commissioners, and to keep in his office a full and correct transcript of such boundaries. In case the boundaries of districts are conflicting, or are incorrectly described, he shall change, harmonize and describe them, and make a report of such action to the commissioners; and on being ratified by the commissioners the boundaries and descriptions so made shall be the legal boundaries and descriptions of the districts of that county. The county superintendent shall furnish the several district clerks with descriptions of the boundaries of their respective districts.

Section 1742. The county superintendent may provide for himself a suitable office for the transaction of official business, when not provided therewith by the county commissioners, and said commissioners shall audit and pay his reasonable accounts for the use and furniture of said office. They shall also furnish him with all necessary stationery and postage; Provided, that not more than one hundred and twenty-five dollars a year shall be paid by any county for office rent, stationery, postage and furniture; Provided, further, That when an office room is furnished by the county he shall not exceed fifty dollars a year for stationery and postage.

Section 1743. No county superintendent shall engage in teaching during his term of office.

Section 1744. No person shall be deemed legally qualified for the office of county superintendent unless he or she holds a certificate of the highest county grade, is a citizen of the United States, has resided one year next preceding the election in this State and one year in the county in which he is a candidate and has had twelve months successful experience in teaching in the public schools of this State. Provided, That in case a certificate held by any of the present incumbents of the office of county superintendents shall expire during the term of such superintendent, such person may apply to the superintendent of the the nearest county for a certificate, as provided by law; and in case a certificate shall be refused the party feeling grieved thereby may appeal to the Superintendent of Public Instruction, who may, upon examination of said person, determine whether a certificate shall be granted.

ARTICLE III.
SCHOOL DISTRICTS.

Sec.		Sec.	
1750.	School District Defined.	1755.	District in Two Counties.
1751.	Organization of New District.	1756.	District Deprived of Apportionment in certain cases.
1752.	District Boundaries.		
1753.	Apportionment of Moneys to New Districts.	1757.	Same.
		1758.	Same.
1754.	Division of District Funds and Property.	1759.	Powers as Body Corporate.
		1760.	When District May be Created.

Section 1750. The term "school district," as used in this title is declared to mean the territory under the jurisdiction of a single board, designated as "board of trustees," and shall be organized in form and manner as hereinafter provided, and shall be known as district No.———— of————county: Provided, That all school districts now existing, as shown by the records of the County Superintendents, are hereby recognized as legally organized districts.

Section 1751. For the purpose of organizing a new district, a petition in writing shall be made to the county superintendent, signed by the parents or guardians of at least ten census children, between the ages of six and twenty-one years, residing within the boundaries of the proposed new district, and residing at a greater distance than two miles from any school house, which petition shall describe the boundaries of the proposed new district, and give the names of all children of school age residing within the boundaries of the proposed new district, at the date of presenting said petition. The county superintendent shall give notice to parties interested by posting notices at least ten days prior to the time appointed by him for considering said petition, in at least three of the most public places in the proposed new district , and one on the school house then in one of the most public places of said old district, and shall on the day fixed in the notice proceed to hear said petition, and if he deem it advisable to grant the petition he shall make an order establishing said district and describing the boundaries thereof, from which order an appeal may be taken by three resident taxpayers of said new district to the board of county commissioners within thirty days, and their decision shall be final; Provided, That should the county superintendent refuse to make an order establishing said new district an appeal may be taken by three resident taxpayers of said new district in the manner hereinbefore described.

Section 1752. The boundaries of any district cannot be changed except in forming new districts, unless a majority of heads of families residing on the territory which it is proposed to transfer or include present a petition in writing to the county superintendent, which petition shall describe the change which it is proposed to have made. It shall also state the reason for desiring said change and the number of children of school age residing on the territory to be transferred or included. The county superintendent shall file said petition in his office, and shall give notice to parties interested by posting notices at least ten days prior to the time appointed for considering said petition, one of which shall be in a public place in the territory which it is proposed shall be annexed or transferred, and one on the door of the school house in each district affected by the change, or if there be no school house in such district, then in some public place of each district effected by the proposed change, or if there be no place in such district or districts, and at the time stated in said notices he shall proceed to hear said petition and if he deem it advisable, he shall grant the same and make an order fixing the boundaries, and unless an appeal be taken to the board of county commissioners within thirty days upon a hearing thereof the decision of said board shal lbe final. All of the papers, documents, and records in the case shall be certified to the county commisioners for their determination of the matter on appeal; Provided, That two or more districts lying contiguous may upon a petition of a majority of the heads of families residing in each of said district presented to the county superintendent in writing, be united to constitute but one district; Provided, further, That joint districts, (districts lying partly in one county and partly in another) may be formed in the same manner as other new districts are formed, except that the petition herein provided for must be made to the county superintendent of each county affected; but in the case of joint districts, all of the provisions herein enumerated for the formation of a new district must be by concurrent action of the superintendent of each county affected.

Section 1753. No new district formed by the sub-division of an old one shall be entitled to any share of public money belonging to the old district, until a school has actually been taught one month in the new district, and unless within eight months from the order of the county superintendent granting such new district, a school is opened, the action making a new district shall be void, and all elections or appointments of trustees or clerks made in consequence of such action, and all rights and office of parties so elected or appointed shall cease and determine.

Section 1754. When a new district is formed from one or more old ones, the school funds remaining to the credit of the district, after providing for all outstanding debts, excepting debts incurred for building and furnishing school houses, shall be divided as follows: The basis for the division of the school fund shall be the school population, as shown by the last school census before the division of the district or districts occurred, and shall apply to such funds as remain to the credit of said old district or districts at the time of the organization of said new district, and said district shall receive funds in proportion to its per cent of the said census. In case of division, each district shall own and hold all permanent property, such as sites, school houses and furniture situated within its boundaries. All division of funds under this provision shall be made by the county superintendent, and when there are unpaid special taxes on the county tax book, belonging to a district at a date of its division, the county treasurer, upon being notified of such division by the county superintendent, shall retain all money received in payment of such special tax, until the same shall be apportioned by the county superintendent, whose duty it shall be to apportion said money quarterly, between the fractions of the divided district, according to the location of the property on which said tax was levied. At the first apportionment after the organization of a new district, the county superintendent shall apportion to such district its per capita proportion of the general fund, but no money, either from the general or special fund, shall be paid out of the county treasury on account of such district until a school shall have been taught therein one month.

Section 1755. Whenever a district lies partly in one county and partly in another, the county superintendent must apportion to such district such proportion of the school money to which such district is entitled as the number of school census children residing in that portion of the district situate in his county bears to the whole number of school census children in the whole district. The trustees and teachers of joint districts must make to the superintendent of each county in which the district is located the reports which other trustees and teachers are required to make, and also the number of pupils attending the school from each county; and all other acts which from their nature should be separately kept and done, as if each portion of said joint district belonging to each county were an entire district in the respective counties. The teachers of such joint districts shall have certificates from the superintendent of the county in which the school house is located.

Section 1756. The school trustees or school board of any district who shall employ any teacher in the public schools of their district for a period of more than three months or who shall not hold a legal certificate of fitness for the occupation of teaching, in full force and effect, shall be deemed guilty of a misdemeanor. Provided, That this section shall not apply to such trustees as do not consent to such employment.
(Sec. 1756. Act approved March 8th, 1897.)

Section 1757. No school district shall be entitled to receive any apportionment of any school moneys which shall not have maintained a free school for at least three months during the next preceding school year; provided, that any new district, formed by the division of an old one, shall be entitled to its apportionment where the time that school was maintained in the old district before division and in the new one after division shall be equal to at least three months.

Section 1758. The trustees of any school districts using text-books other than those prescribed by law, (except for supplementary purposes) shall be deemed guilty of a misdemeanor. Provided, That the foregoing shall only apply to those trustees consenting to the use of such other books.
(Sec. 1758. Act approved March 8th, 1897.)

Sec. 1759. Every school district constituted and formed as provided in this act shall be and is hereby, declared to be a body corporate, and under its own proper name or number as such corporate body may sue and be sued, contract and be contracted with, and may require, purchase and hold and use personal or real property for school purposes for the purpose mentioned in this act and sell and dispose of the same.

Section 1760. No school district shall be created between the first day of March and the first day of September following of each year.

ARTICLE IV.
ELECTION OF SCHOOL TRUSTEES.

Sec.		Sec.	
1770.	Election, number and term.	1779.	Challenge. Oath.
1771.	Board of County Commissioners supervise election.	1780.	Poll and tally lists.
		1781.	Certificate of election.
1772.	Notices of election. Judges.	1782.	Trustees must qualify.
1773.	Polling places.	1783.	Who eligible for trustee.
1774.	Judges of election.	1784.	Registry precincts. Agents.
1775.	Opening of polls.	1785.	Arrangement of precincts. Check lists.
1776.	Publication of notice of election.		
1777.	Qualifications of electors.	1786.	Expenses of election. How paid.
1778.	Ballots. Form of.	1787.	Bonds of trustees. Compensation.

Section 1770. An annual election for the election of school trustees shall be held in each school district in the state on the first Saturday in April in each year, at the district school house if there be one, and if there be none, at a place designated by the board of trustees or the county commissioners as the case may be. All districts having a population of twelve thousand or more are, and hereafter shall be, districts of the first class. All districts having a population of one thousand and less than twelve thousand are and shall hereafter be districts of the second class, and all districts having a population of less than one thousand are and hereafter shall be districts of the third class. In districts of the first class the number of trustees shall be seven and in districts of the second class the number of trustees shall be five and in districts of the third class the number of trustees shall be three. In school districts having a population of over twenty thousand people, any trustee at the time of the passage of this act, save those who are serving by appointment to fill vacancies, shall continue to hold for the term of two years from the third Saturday in the month of April of the year in which they were elected, and those filling vacancies until the third Saturday in April, 1899, and at all subsequent elections one or more trustees as the case may be must be elected, who shalll each serve for a term of two years or until their successors are elected or appointd and shall have qualified. A vacancy in the office of school trustee must be fillled by appointment by the County Superintendent of Schools, subject to confirmation by a majority of the remaining members of said Board, if those remaining constitute a majority of the total of said Board.

(Sec. 1770. Act approved March 6th, 1897, as amended by an Act approved March 3d, 1899.)

Section 1771. In districts of the first class the election shall be under the supervision of the Board of County Commissioners of the county in which the same are situated, and shall be held and conducted as hereinafter provided.

Section 1771. Act approved March 6th, 1897.)

Section 1772. In districts of the second and third classes, the election of school trustees shall be held and conducted under the supervision of the Board of School Trustees. The clerk of the school district must, not less than fifteen days before the election required under this act, post notices in three public places in said district, and in incorporated cities in each ward, which notices must specify the time and place of election, and the hours during which the polls will be open. The trustees must appoint by an order entered in their records, three qualified electors of said district, to act as judges at such election, and the clerk of the district shall notify them, by mail of their appointment. Said judges shall appoint one of their number to act as clerk at such election. If the judges named are not present at the time for opening the polls, the electors present may appoint judges and the judges so appointed shall designate one of their number to act as clerk.

In the districts of the second and third classes, having fifty or more children of school age, the names of all the candidates for membership on the School Board must be received and filed by the clerk and posted at each polling place at least five days next preceding the election.

Any five qualified electors of the districts may file with the clerk the nominations of as many persons as are to be elected to the School Board at the ensuing election.

(Sec. 1772. As amended by Act approved Feb. 28th, 1899.)

"Section 1773. The Board of County Commissioners shall, at least thirty days before the annual election of school trustees, by an order entered upon the minutes of their meeting, designate and establish a suitable number of polling places, and create an equal number of election precincts to correspond, and define the boundaries thereof."

(Sec. 1773. Act approved March 3, 1899 amending act of March 6, 1897.)

Section 1774. The board of County Commissoners shall, at least ten days before the day of annual election for trustees in any district of the first class, appoint three qualified electors of the district for each polling place established, to act as judges of election, and the County Clerk shall notify such persons by mail of their appointment. Such judges shall designate one of their number to act as clerk at such election. If the judges appointed or any of them are not present at the time for the opening of the polls, the electors present may appoint judges, who must be qualified electors to act in the place of those who are absent. The County Clerk shall, at least fifteen days before the election required to be held under this Act, in districts of the first class, give notice of the election to be held in all said districts, by posting a notice thereof in three public places in the district, and in incorporated cities and towns in each ward, which notices must specify the time and place of election, the number of trustees to be elected, and the hours during which the polls will be open.

(Sec. 1774. Act approved March 6, 1897.)

Section 1775. In districts of the first class the polls must be opened at eight o'clock A. M. and kept open until twelve o'clock M. and from one o'clock P. M. until eight o'clock P. M. In districts of the second and third classes the polls may be opened for such length of time as the board of trustees may order: Provided that, such polls must be kept open from two o'clock P. M. to six o'clock P. M.

(Sec. 1775. Act approved March 6, 1897.)

Section 1776. Whenever in the judgment of the board of county commissioners the best interests of the district will be served by the publication of such notices of election in some newspaper in the county, they may, by an order entered on the minutes of their meeting, direct the County Clerk to publish the notice of election required to be given in districts of the first class in some newspaper in the county.

(Sec. 1776. Act approved March 6, 1897.)

Section 1777. Every citizen of the United States who has resided in the State of Montana for one year, and thirty days in the school district next preceding the election, may vote thereat. Women of the age of twenty-one years and upwards who are citizens of the United State, and who have resided in the State of Montana one year, and in school district for thirty days next preceding the day of election, may vote thereat: Provided however that before any such person shall be entitled to vote in any district of the first class, he or she shall have registered as in this Act hereinafter required.

(Sec. 1777. Act approved March 6, 1897.)

Section 1778. The voting must be by ballot, without reference to the general election laws in regard to nominations, form of ballot, or manner of voting in districts of the second and third classes. But in districts of the first class the ballot shall show the name or names of the candidates and the length for which they are to be elected. These ballots shall be as near as possible in the following form.

FOR SCHOOL TRUSTEES.
For three (3) year term.

VOTE FOR THREE.

JOHN ABNER
WILLIAM BROWN
ADAM SMITH

For one (1) year term.

VOTE FOR ONE.

GEORGE DAVIS

In districts of the first class no person shall be voted for or elected as trustees, unless he or she has been nominated therefor by a bona fide public meeting held in the district at least ten days before the day of election, and at which at least twenty qualified electors were present, and a chairman and a secretary were elected, and a certificate of such nomination setting forth the place where the meeting was held, giving the names of the candidates in full, and if there are different terms to be filled, the term for which such candidate was nominated, duly certified by the chairman and secretary of such meeting, shall be filed with the county clerk at least eight days before the day of election. The nomination and election of any person shall be void, unless he or she was nominated at a meeting as above provided at which at least twenty qualified electors were present, and his or her nomination certified and filed as aforesaid, and the county commissioners shall not count any votes cast for any person, unless he or she has been so nominated and a certificate thereof filed as herein required. The county commissioners shall cause to be printed ballots of the form aforesaid, on which shall appear the names of all persons who were regularly nominated and whose certificate of nomination was properly filed as aforesaid. In district of the first class the person desiring to vote shall, at the time he or she presents his or her ballot, announce his or her name, and the judges of election if they find such name on the official check list, or if not and he or she takes the oath herein prescribed, one of the judges shall take the ballot and deposit it in the ballot box, and the clerk shall immediately write the name of such person on the poll list and one of the judges shall write opposite the said name on the official check lists the word "voted." Any person voting at such election who is not entitled to vote, and any person voting more than once thereat, shall be guilty of a misdemeanor and shall be punished accordingly; and any person taking a false oath, shall be guilty of perjury. No person shall be entitled to vote at any election for school trustees in any district of the first class, unless his or her name shall, on the day of election, appear on the official check list furnished by the county clerk to the judges of election: Provided, however, that if any person, otherwise qualified to vote, makes oath before one of the judges that he or she registered at any registry precinct in such district, naming it, before a registry agent giving his name, to vote at said election, and that his or her name does not appear correctly on said check list, or has been omitted therefrom, or that by reason of absence or sickness during the period of registration he or she was unable to register, the judges of election shall make an entry opposite his or her name on the poll list to the effect that he or she was sworn and voted, and shall permit him or her to vote. The county commissioners shall provide for each election of trustees double as many ballots as there are voters registered within such district. No other ballot than that provided by the county commissioners shall be received by the judges and in districts of the first class, where a daily paper is issued, the commissioners shall cause to be published in at least one paper for three days preceding the election, such official ballot, and in such districts where there is no daily paper, but a weekly, the official ballot shall be printed at least once in a weekly paper. Trustees must provide in each polling place designated by them a sufficient number of booths, placed, or compartments, which must be furnished with such supplies as shall enable the elector to conveniently prepare his or her ballot, and in which electors screened from observation must mark their ballots. Guard railing must be so constructed that only persons within such railing and officers of election can approach within ten feet of the ballot boxes or the booths herein provided. Before delivering any ballot to an elector the judges must print on the back and near the top of the ballot, with a rubber stamp, the designation "official ballot." Each qualified elector shall receive from the judge one ballot. The elector on receiving his or her ballot must forthwith without leaving the polling place, and within the guarded rail provided, and alone, retire to one of the booths or compartments, and prepare his or her ballot, by marking a cross before the name of each candidate for whom he or she desires to vote. After preparing his or her ballot the elector must fold it so that the face of the ballot will be concealed, and so that the endorsement stamped there-

on may be seen. He or she must then vote forthwith, and before leaving the polling place. Any elector who, because of physical disability or inability to read the English language is unable to mark his ballot, may request one of the judges to help him or her. Any elector who, by accident or mistake spoils his or her ballot, may on returning the spoiled ballot receive another.
(Sec. 1778. Act approved March 6, 1897.)

Section 1779. Any person offering to vote may be challenged by any elector of the district, and the judges must thereupon administer to the person challenged an oath in substance as follows: You do solemnly swear that you are a citizen of the United States; that you are twenty-one years of age; and that you have resided in this State one year, and in this school district thirty days next preceding this election, and that you have not voted this day. So help you God. If he or she is a resident of a district of the second or third class, and he or she takes this oath, his or her vote must be received; otherwise rejected. If he or she is a resident of a district of the first class and takes this oath, and has complied with the provisions of this Act, with reference to elections therein or complies herewith, his or her vote must be received; otherwise it shall be rejected. Any person who shall swear falsely before any registry agent or judge of election, shall be guilty of perjury and shall be punished accordingly.
(Sec. 1779. Act approved March 6, 1897.)

Section 1780. At every election held under this Act, in districts of the first class, a poll and tally list shall be kept by the judges and clerk at each polling place, and immediately after the close of the polls the judges shall count the ballots, and if there be more ballots than votes cast the judges must draw by lot from the ballots without seeing them, a sufficient number of ballots to make the ballots remaining correspond with the number of votes cast. The clerk shall write down in alphabetical order in a poll book provided for that purpose the name of every person voting, at the time he or she deposits his or her ballot. There shall also be provided a tally list for each polling place; after the ballots have been counted and made to agree with the poll list, the judges shall proceed to count them. The clerk shall enter in the tally list the name of every person voted for trustee, and the term, and tally opposite his or her name, the number of votes cast for him or her and at the end thereof set down in a column provided for that purpose the whole number of votes he or she has received. The judges and clerk shall sign a certificate to said tally list setting forth the whole number of votes cast for each person or trustee, designating the term, and they shall verify the same as being correct to the best of their knowledge

before an officer authorized to administer oaths. No informality in such certificate shall vitiate the election, if the number of votes received for each person can reasonably be ascertained from said tally list. In districts of the second and third class said books and tally lists shall be returned to the board of trustees of the district, who shall canvass the vote and cause the clerk of district, to issue certificates of election to the person or persons elected, designating their term, a copy of which must be forwarded to the county superintendent of schools. In districts of the first class said poll books and the tally lists shall be delivered to the county clerk, and the board of county commissioners shall canvass the votes. School trustees are hereby authorized to administer oaths to the judges of election, and the oath of office to the trustees elected.
(Sec. 1780. Act approved March 6, 1897.)

Section 1781. The Board of County Commissioners shall canvass the votes of all districts of the first class in the same manner that they are required to canvass the votes at other elections and declare the results. The County Clerk shall thereupon make out and mail to the person or persons elected a certificate of election, stating the term, and shall mail a copy thereof to the county superintendent of schools.
(Sec. 1781. Act approved March 6, 1897.)

Section 1782. Trustees elected shall take office immediately after qualifying and shall hold office for the term of three years and until their successors are elected and qualified, or appointed by the county superintendent of schools and qualified. Every trustee elected shall file his or her oath of office with the county superintendent of schools. Any trustee who shall fail to qualify within fifteen days after being elected shall forfeit all rights to office, and the county superintendent of schools shall appoint to fill the vacancy.
(Sec 1782. Act approved March 6, 1897.)

Section 1783. Any person, male or female, who is a qualified voter at any election under this act, shall be eligible to office of school trustee in such district.
(Sec. 1783. Act approved March 6, 1897.)

Section 1784. The board of county commissioners of every county in which there shall be a school district of the first class shall, at least fifteen days before the school election for the year 1897, and thereafter at least twenty days before the next annual school election, by order entered on the minutes of the board, lay out such district into not less than two nor more than thirty registry precincts as may seem to the board most necessary, and shall define the boundaries thereof, which shall be known as School Registry Precinct No. 1, School Registry Precinct No. 2, and so on. They shall at the same time the registry precincts are established, appoint one person, male or female, qualified to vote at the coming election in such precinct, registry agent for such precinct, and of the number of registry agents appointed, they shall designate one as principal registry agent for said school district. All registry agents shall be appointed annually, and they are hereby authorized and empowered to administer oaths and affirmations, and to do such other acts as may be necessary to carry out the purposes of this Act. Before entering upon the duties prescribed in this Act, the registry agents must severally take and subscribe before an officer authorized to administer oaths the constitutional oath of office, and file the same with the county clerk of their respective counties. The Board of County Commissioners shall designate the place where the office of every registry agent appointed under this Act shall be kept, and they shall cause to be published in a newspaper in the district, or posted in at least three places in each registry precinct, a notice of registration, which shall describe the boundaries of each registry precinct, give the location of the office, and the name of the registry agent therefor, and the date when, and the hours during which the office of the registry agent will be open, and during which persons residing in said precinct may apply and be registered therein. This notice must be published or posted for three days preceding the day when the registration begins, and continued until registration is closed, and shall be issued and signed by the county clerk. Every registry agent appointed under this Act, shall open his office for the purpose of registering votes in his or her district on the tenth day preceding the day of the next annual election for school trustees: Provided, said day be not Sunday or a legal holiday; and should said day be Sunday or a legal holiday, then he or she shall open his or her office on the ninth day next preceding the day of election. He or she shall keep his or her office open between the hours of nine A. M. and twelve M. and one P. M. and five P. M. and from six P. M. until ten P. M. for the period of three days, not including Sunday or a legal holiday and during said time he or she shall register the names of all persons residing in his or her registry precinct, qualified and entitled to vote at the coming election, or who will have a vote thereat under the provisions of this Act. Registry agents shall not sit on Sundays or legal holidays, and while not opened required to register, during the hours of, from twelve to one P. M. and five to six P. M. they may nevertheless do so if they desire, each registry agent shall be provided with an official register. He or she shall enter therein under the proper heading, the number and date of registration the name, with the first or given name in full and the nativity of the elector, together with the number or a particular description of the house, room or building where the elector resides so as to reasonably identify the same. The names shall be entered in alphabetical order the surname being written first. Every person desiring to be registered for such election must apply to the registry agent for the precinct in which he or she shall reside, at his or her office during the hours of registration. No persons shall be registered by any registry agent unless such person is at the time a resident of his or her precinct. Every person applying to the registry agent shall, before he or she shall be entitled to have his or her name registered, take and subscribe to the following oath or affirmation, which shall be administered by the registry agent to-wit: I do solemnly swear or affirm that I am a citizen of the United States, or that I am entitled to become a citizen of the United States, and it is my honest intention to become such before the school election day of this year; and that I am of the age of twenty-one years, and will have actually and not constructively, been a bona fide resident in Montana twelve months, and in the school district thirty days next preceding the day of election, and that I am not registered elsewhere in this school district for this election year, So help me God. The registry books shall be open at all times to the inspection of any electors of the district.

(Sec. 1784. Act approved March 6, 1897.)

Section 1785. The county commissioners in establishing the voting precincts and registry precincts shall so arrange them that each voting precinct in which a polling place shall be established shall be composed of a certain number of designated registry precincts. On the next day succeeding that on which the rgistration is closed each registry agent shall deliver to the county clerk of his or her county his or her official registry duly certified by himself or herself. The principal registry agent of each district shall immediately enter upon the work of making therefrom official check lists. He or she shall copy into books to be provided for that purpose and to be known as the official check lists for each election precinct, designating the number of the voting precinct thereon, all the names in alphabetical order contained in the several official registers which have been returned from the several registry precincts within said voting precinct, together with the other entries contained in the official registers and shall complete the making of one official check list in such manner for each election or voting precinct which has been established, within five days. The county commissioners shall allow him or her such assistance as may be necessary to complete such official check list within such time. When he or she has completed the official list he or she shall verify each of them by his oath that the same is correct according to his or her best

information, knowledge and belief and deliver the same with all official registers to the county clerk who shall on the day of election at or before the time for the polls to open, deliver the official check list for each election precinct or polling place to one of the judges thereof at such polling place.
(Sec. 1785. Act approved March 6, 1897.)

Section 1786. All the expenses necessarily incurred in the matter of holding elections for school trustees shall be paid out of the school funds of the district. For districts of the first class the county commissioners shall provide all the stationery, books and supplies and all bills and claims therefor and for the expenses of such election shall be presented to and allowed by the board of County Commissioners when audited by the County Auditor as other claims, and said board shall thereupon cause the same to be certified and delivered by the County Clerk to the proper board of school trustees, who shall cause the same to be paid out of the school funds of the district as other school expenses are paid. All registry agents shall receive the sum of four dollars per day each for the time which they shall be engaged in work of registration; judges of election in districts of the first class shall receive not to exceed five dollars per day each for all services connected with the election. Judges of election in other districts shall receive no compensation. The compensation hereby provided shall be paid in the same manner as other claims.
(Sec. 1786. Act approved March 6, 1897.)

Section 1787. Every School Trustee in a district of the first class provided said District shall have a population not less than twenty thousand, shall give an official bond in the sum of ten thousand dollars, for the faithful discharge of his or her duties, which bond shall be approved by the District Judge and filed with the County Clerk, and every such trustee shall be entitled to receive out of the school funds of the district the sum of four dollars for each meeting of trustees, which he or she shall attend in giving the necessary attention to school business, not exceeding however one meeting each week, and he or she shall receive no compensation for his attendance at any meeting unless he or she attends throughout its entire session. The compensation here provided shall be audited and allowed by the Board of Trustees and entered upon their records.
(Sec. 1787. Act amending Act of March 6, 1897, approved March 3, 1899.)

ARTICLE V.
BOARD OF TRUSTEES.

Sec.		Sec.	
1790.	Powers. Quorum.	1805.	Misdemeanor. Penalty.
1791.	Term.	1806.	Repayment of loans.
1792.	Trustees of new district.	1807.	Must procure American flags.
1793.	Meetings. Organization. Clerk.	1808.	Flags to be displayed.
1794.	Meetings, general.	1809.	Expenses of flags.
1795.	Financial statement.	1810.	Powers concerning bonds.
1796.	Chairman. Rules.	1811.	Disposal of proceeds of bonds.
1797.	Powers and duties.	1812.	District responsible on bonds.
1798.	Duties concerning privies.	1813.	Must levy tax for interest, etc.
1799.	Same.	1814.	Redemption of bonds.
1800.	Penalty.	1815.	Payment of interest.
1801.	Power over property.	1816.	Preparation of bonds.
1802.	Shall not be interested in contracts.	1817.	Felony. Penalty.
1803.	Liability.	1818.	Surplus money used for building.
1804.	May establish high schools.		

Section 1790. Except when otherwise authorized by law, every school district is under the control of a board of school trustees consisting of three members, a majority of which constitute a quorum for the transaction of business.

Section 1791. The term of office of school trustees is three years, from the third Saturday in April next succeeding their election.

Section 1792. When a new district is organized, such trustees of the old as reside within the limits of the new one shall be trustees in the new district, and the county superintendent must appoint the remaining trustees for the new and old districts, who shall hold office until the next annual school election.

Section 1793. The School Trustees shall meet annually on the third Saturday in April, and organize by choosing one of their number chairman, and a competent person, not a member of the Board as Clerk. In districts of the first class, the clerk before entering upon the duties of his office, shall be required to give an official bond in the sum of ten thousand dollars conditioned for the faithful performance of his duties and to be approved and filed as other official bonds.

Section 1794. The Board shall hold, in districts of the first class, at least one and not more than five meetings each month, for the transaction of its business; and in all districts at least four meetings each year shall be held, to-wit: On the third Saturdays of April, July, October and January at such places and hours as shall be fixed by the Board. A special meeting of the Board may be held upon the call of the chairman, or of any two members of the board. At least forty-eight hours written notice shall be given to each member of the Board

of any special meeting, and no business transaction by the Board shall be valid unless transacted at a regular or special meeting thereof.
(Secs. 1793-1794. Act approved March 3, 1899.)

Section 1795. In school districts in which the funds shall equal or exceed $25,000 in each year, there shall be published in the newspaper which has contracted to do the public printing in the county in which the district is located between the first and tenth days of June of each year, and between the first and tenth days of December of each year, a financial statement, covering the six preceding months, showing in detail the amount of money received, the amount paid out and for what purpose it was so paid, and the balance in the county treasurer's hands to the credit of the district at the time of the making of the statement. The costs of such publication shall be paid by order of the board of school trustees out of their respective school funds, and the prices paid must not exceed per folio that allowed by the county commissioners for the publication of the financial statement of the county treasurer.

Section 1796. The chairman shall preside at all the meetings of the board, and shall perform such duties as usually pertain to such office and in accordance with the customary rules of order.

Section 1797. Every school board unless otherwise especially provided by law, shall have power and it shall be its duty:

1. To prescribe and enforce rules not inconsistent with law, or those prescribed by the Superintendent of Public Instruction for their own government of schools under their supervision.

2. To employ or discharge teachers, mechanics or laborers and to fix and order paid their wages; to determine the rate of tuition of nonresident pupils, and to fix the compensation to be allowed the clerk for the time necessarily spent in the service of the district, as required by law, or as directed by the board.

3. To enforce the rules and regulations of the superintendent of public instruction for the government of schools, pupils and teacher and to enforce the course of study.

4. To provide for school furniture and for everything needed in the school house or for the use of the school board.

5. To rent, repair and insure school houses.

6. To build or remove school houses and to purchase or sell school lots when directed by a vote of the district so to do.

7. To hold in trust for their district all real or personal property, for the benefit of the school thereof.

8. To suspend or expel pupils from school who refuse to obey the rules thereof, and to exclude from school, children under six years of age where the interest of the school requires such exclusion.

9. To provide books for indigent children on the written statement of the teacher that the parents of such children are not able to purchase them.

10. To require all pupils to be furnished with suitable books as a condition of membership in the school.

11. To exclude from school and school libraries, all books, tracts, papers and other publications of immoral and pernicious nature.

12. To require teachers to conform to the law.

13. To make an annual report, as required by law, to the county superintendent on or before the first day of October in each year, in the manner and form and on the blanks prescribed and furnished by the superintendent of public instruction.

14. To make a report directly to the superintendent of public instruction whenever instructed by him to do so.

15. Whenever a pupil resident in one district desires to attend school in an adjoining district, such pupil shall be permitted to do so, Provided,that the board may refuse pupils from such dstrict upon the ground of insufficient room. That the board of trustees shall have power to transfer the school moneys due by apportionment to such pupils to the district in which they may attend school; and provided further, That where any pupil lives five miles or more from the school in his district such pupil shall have the right to attend any school which is nearer upon petition to the county superintendent. When such petition is made to the county superintendent he or she shall keep a record of the same on file in his office.

16. To determine what branches, if any, in addition to those required by law shall be taught in any school in the district, subject to the approval of the county superintendent.

17. To visit every school in their district at least once in each term and to examine carefully into its management, condition and want. This clause applies to each of the trustees.

18. To provide for each school house separate out houses for the sexes.

(Sec. 1797. Act approved March 8, 1897.)

Section 1798. It is hereby made the duty of the school trustees of all school districts in this State to provide separate privies or outhouses for the use of the sexes at all school houses where the same do not exist, and to see that the same are kept in good repair, and in a clean condition. Such privies or outhouses must be located and built in such a manner as to secure privacy. In all cases where there is no fence dividing the play yards of the sexes the privies or outhouses herein named shall be separate and distinct buildings, and situated at least twenty feet apart.

Section 1799. It shall be the duty of all trustees, teachers, janitor or janitors of school districts to see that all privies or outhouses are kept in good repair and in a clean condition.

Section 1800. Any trustee or trustees, teacher, janitor or janitors failing to comply with the provisions of this act shall be deemed guilty of a misdemeanor and upon conviction thereof shall be fined in a sum not exceeding one hundred dollars or imprisoned in the county jail not exceeding ninety days or both such fine and imprisonment in the discretion of the court.

Section 1801. The board of trustees for each school district shall have custody of all school property belonging to the district, and shall have power in the name of the district or in their own names as trustees of the district, to convey by deed all the interest of their district in or to any school house or lot directed to be sold by vote of the district, and all conveyances of real estate made to the district, or to the trustees thereof, shall be made to the board of trustees of the district and to their successors in office; said board in the name of the district shall have power to transact all business necessary for maintaining schools and protecting the rights of the district.

Section 1802. It shall be unlawful for any trustee to have any pecuniary interest, either directly or indirectly, in any erection of school houses, or for warming, ventilating, furnishing or repairing the same, or to be in any manner connected with the furnishing of supplies for the maintenance of the schools or to receive or to accept any compensation or reward for services rendered as trustee.

Section 1803. Any board of trustees shall be liable as trustees, in the name of the district, for any judgment against the district, for any salary due any teacher on contract, and for all debts legally contracted under the provisions of this title, and they shall pay such judgments or liabilities out of the school moneys to the credit of such district.

Section 1804. Whenever the interests of the district requires it the board of trustees may establish a high school, employ a principal teacher and subordinate teachers, and grade the school into departments and classes.

Section 1805. When any school officer is suspended by election or otherwise he shall immediately deliver to his successor in office all books, papers and moneys pertaining to his office; and such officer who shall refuse to do so, or who shall wilfully mutilate or destroy any such books or papers, or any part thereof, or shall misapply any moneys entrusted to him by virtue of his office, shall be guilty of a misdemeanor, and shall be punished by a fine, in the discretion of the court, not exceeding one hundred dollars.

Section 1806. Whenever heretofore money has been loaned or advanced to the board of school trustees of any school district for the erection of a school house or school houses therein by any person or corporation in reliance upon the proceeds of the sales of bonds for the repayment of the same, the issuance of which bonds have been voted for by a majority of the electors of such district, voting at an election held for the purpose of authorizing the issuance of the same for the erection of a school house or school houses, which said money has been used by such board of school trustees in the erection of a school house or school houses in such district, but which bonds when issued have been adjudged and held to be void or invalid by the Supreme Court of the state, the money so loaned or advanced may be repaid, together with interest thereon covering the period for which interest has not been paid, at the rate specified in said bonds so held to be void; said payment to be made by the board of school trustees to the person or corporation who or which had loaned or advanced the same, from the proceeds of the sale of any bonds thereafter issued for the purpose of building one or more school houses in said district, or for any other school purposes.

Section 1807. That the trustees of the several school districts of the State of Montana shall, within ninety days from the passage of this act, procure by purchase or donation, an American flag with accompanying necessary poles and ropes, etc., for each and every school house in their respective districts. Said flags shall be of dimensions not less than four by six feet, and they shall be made from durable material.

Section 1808. It shall be the duty of the school trustees to cause said flags to be displayed over such school houses every day, during the sessions thereof, provided the weather is such as to permit the display without injury to the flags.

Section 1809. The school trustees are hereby authorized and empowered to use such portion of the school funds as remain in their hands and which is not othewise appropriated, for the purchase and erection of the flags, poles, etc.

Section 1810. The school trustees of any school district of the State of Montana, shall have and are hereby given in addition to the power already conferred on them, authority to issue on the credit of their respective districts, coupon bonds (and sell the same), for the purpose of providing the necessary funds to pay maturing bonds under the following conditions, to-wit:

First—When there is not sufficient money to the credit of the school district applicable to pay said maturing bonds.

Second—When in the judgment of the school trustees to levy and collect a special tax for the purpose of paying said maturing bonds, would be a hardship and a burden to the school district.

Third—All bonds issued under the provisions of this act shall bear upon their face the words, "Refunding School Bonds," and shall also recite in the body of the bond that "This bond is issued for the purpose of providing funds to pay maturing and outstanding bonds."

Fourth—Said bonds shall bear interest at a rate not exceeding six per cent per annum (and interest may be payable semi-annually) and payable and redeemable within a period not to exceed twenty years from the date of issue; Provided, That such issue of bonds shall not exceed in amount the face value of the bonds they are issued to replace, and Provided further that such reissue shall not be made more than once upon any indebtedness.

Fifth—The trustees shall fix the denomination, term, rate and form of said bonds not inconsistent with the requirements hereinbefore set forth; and may issue and sell such bonds at any time when deemed necessary and expedient to preserve and maintain the credit of their respective school districts; Provided, however, that said school trustees shall be required to first submit the question of issuing said bonds to the electors of said school districts as required in the case of issuing other bonds.

Sixth—Said bonds shall be advertised for sale in not less than one newspaper of general circulation, published in the State of Montana, for a period of not less than four weeks preceding the date fixed for sale of said bonds; said advertisement shall briefly describe the bonds, stating the time when, and place where said sale will take place; Provided, That said bonds shall not be sold at less than their par value, and the trustees are authorized to reject any bids and sell said bonds at private sale, if they deem it for the best interests of the district to do so.

Seventh—Said bonds and coupons (attached), shall be signed by the chairman of the board of trustees, and the school clerk of the district; Provided, a lithographic or engraved fac simile of the signatures of the chairman and clerk may be affixed to the coupons only when so recited in the bond.

Eighth—Each bond so issued shall be registered by the county treasurer of the county wherein such school district is located, in a book provided for the purpose, which shall show the date, number, term and amount of each bond, and the person or persons to whom the bonds are issued or sold.

Section 1811. All moneys arising from the sale of said bonds shall be paid forthwith into the treasury of the county in which said school district is located, and shall be immediately available to apply for the purpose authorized and no other purpose.

Section 1812. The faith of each school district is solemnly pledged for the payment of the interest and the redemption of the principal of the bonds which shall be issued under this act. And for the purpose of enforcing the provisions of this act, each school district shall be a body corporate, which may sue and be sued by, or in the name of, the board of school trustees of such district.

Section 1813. The school trustees of each district shall ascertain the amount of levy annually, a tax necessary to pay the interest, when it becomes due, and provide a sinking fund to redeem the bonds at their maturity; and said tax shall become a lien upon the property in said school district and be collected in the same manner as other taxes for school purposes.

Section 1814. When the sum in said sinking fund shall equal or exceed the amount of any bond then due, the county treasurer shall post in his office a notice that he will, within thirty days from the date of such notice, redeem the bonds then payable, giving the number thereof, and the bonds bearing the lowest number shall be redeemed first, in their order; and Provided, that such redemption shall be made at some regular interest period as set forth in the bond; and if at the expiration of the said thirty days, the holder or holders of said bonds shall fail or neglect to present the same for payment, interest thereon shall cease; but the treasurer shall at all times thereafter be ready to redeem the same on presentation, and when any bond or bonds shall be so purchased or redeemed, the county treasurer shall cancel all bonds so purchased and redeemed, by writing or stamping across the face of such bond or bonds, in ink the words, "Redeemed and Cancelled," and the date of such redemption. And the bonds paid shall be exhibited to the board of county commissioners at their first meeting thereafter.

Section 1815. The county treasurer shall pay out of any moneys belonging to the school district, the interest upon any bonds issued by authority of this act, by such district, when the same shall become due, upon the presentation at his office, of the proper coupon, which shall show the amount due, and the number of the bond to which it belongs; and all coupons so paid shall be cancelled and exhibited to the board of county commissioners at their first meeting thereafter.

Section 1816. The school trustees of any school district shall cause to be printed or lithographed, at the lowest rate, suitable bonds with the coupons attached, when the same shall become necessary and pay therefor out of any moneys in the county treasury to the credit of said school district.

Section 1817. If any of the school trustees of any district shall fail or refuse to pay into the proper county treasury the money arising from the sale of any bonds provided for by this act, they shall be deemed guilty of a felony and upon conviction thereof, shall be punished by imprisonment in the State penitentiary for a term of not less than one year, nor more than ten years.

Section 1818. County school moneys may be used by the county superintendent and trustees for the various purposes as authorized and provided in this article, and for no other purpose, except that in any district, any surplus in the general school fund to the credit of said district, after providing for the expenses of not less than eight months' school may, on a vote of the qualified electors of said district, be used for the purpose of building and improvement. If any school money shall be paid by the authority of the board of trustees for any purpose not authorized by this section, the trustees consenting to such payment shall be liable to the district for the repayment of such sum and a suit to recover the same may be brought by the county attorney or if he shall refuse to bring the same, a suit may be brought by any taxpaying elector in the district.

ARTICLE VI.
DISTRICT CLERKS.
Sec. 1830. Duties Compensation.

Section 1830. The duties of the district clerk shall be as follows:

1. To attend all meetings of the board of trustees; but if he shall not be present, the board of trustees shall select one of their number as

a clerk who shall certify the proceedings of the meeting to the clerk of the district, to be recorded by him. He shall keep his record in a book to be furnished by the board of trustees and he shall preserve a copy of all reports made to the county superintendent and safely preserve and keep all books and documents belonging to his office, and shall turn the same over to his successors.

2. To keep accurate and detailed accounts of all receipts and expenditures of school moneys. At each annual school meeting the district clerk shall present his record book for public inspection and shall make a statement of the financial condition of the district and of the action of the trustees and such record must always be open to public inspection.

3. To make annually, between the first and twentieth days of August of each year, an exact census of all the children and youth between the ages of six and twenty-one years residing in the district and shall specify the number and sex of such children and the names of their parents or guardians. He shall take specifically and separately, a census of all children under six years of age and shall specify the number and sex of such children. All children under twenty-one years of age who may be absent from home for any cause shall be included by the district clerk in this census list of the city, town or district in which their parents reside. He shall make a full report thereof on the blanks furnished for this purpose under oath to the county superintendent thereafter, and, deliver a copy to the school trustees. For taking the census the district clerk shall be paid by the board of trustees, from the county school money to the credit of the district, in the same manner as other contingent expenses are paid, at a rate not exceeding ten cents for each child's name returned by him. He shall receive such other compensation for other services as may be allowed by the board of trustees. In case any district clerk shall fail to take the census provided in this act, at the proper time and if through such neglect the district shall fail to receive its apportionment of school moneys, said school clerk shall be individually liable to the district for the full amount so lost and it may be recovered on a suit brought by any citizen of such district in the name of and for the benefit of the district.

(Sec. 1830. Act approved March 8, 1897.)

ARTICLE VII.
TEACHERS.

Sec.		Sec.	
1840.	Qualifications.	1845.	Duties.
1841.	Teachers' report.	1846.	Penalty.
1842.	Duties.	1847.	Qualification, as to age.
1843.	Construction of teacher's contract.	1848.	Dismissal. Appeal.
1844.	Powers.	1849.	Suspension of teacher's certificate.

Section 1840. No person shall be accounted as a qualified teacher, within the meaning of the school law, who has not first appeared before the county superintendent of the county in which he proposes to teach, and received a certificate setting forth his qualifications; or who has not received a temporary certificate from the county superintendent or has not a State certificate or life diploma from the State Board of Education, or a certificate from some other county, endorsed by the county superintendent: Provided, That special certificates may be granted to persons employed to teach either music, drawing, modern languages or penmanship only.

Section 1841. Every teacher employed in any public school shall make an annual report to the county superintendent on or before the tenth day of September next after the close of each school year, in the form and manner and on the blanks prescribed by the Superintendent of Public Instruction. A copy of such report shall be furnished the district clerk. Any teacher who shall end any school term before the close of the school year shall make a report to the county superintendent immediately after the close of such term, and any teacher who may be teaching any school at the close of the school year, shall, in his or her annual report, include all statistics from the school register for the entire school year notwithstanding any previous report for a part of the year. Teachers shall make such additional reports as shall be required, in pursuance of law, by the Superintendent of Public Instruction. No board of trustees shall draw any order or warrant for the salary of any teacher for the last month of his or her service, until the reports herein required shall have been made and received; Provided, That in all schools acting under the direction of a city superintendent, teachers shall be required to report to such superintendent, whose report shall be accepted by the county superintendent and the trustees in lieu of teachers' reports; and that when there is no city superintendent the report of the principal shall be accepted in lieu of the teachers' reports.

Section 1842. It shall be the duty of the teacher of every public school in this State, to keep, in a neat and business-like manner, a daily register in such form and upon such blanks as shall be prepared by the

Superintendent of Public Instruction, and no board of trustees shall draw any warrant for the salary of any teacher for the last month of his service in the school, at the end of any term or year, until they shall have received a certificate from the district clerk that the said register has been properly kept, the summaries made and the statistics entered, or until by personal examination they shall have satisfied themselves that it has been done.

Teachers shall faithfully enforce in school the course of study and regulations prescribed, and if any teacher shall refuse or neglect to comply with such regulations, then the board of trustees shall be authorized to withhold any warrant for salaries due until such teacher shall comply therewith. No teacher shall be employed except by written order of a majority of the board of trustees, at a regular or special meeting thereof, nor unless the holder of a legal teacher's certificate in full force and effect.

Section 1843. In every contract between any teacher and board of trustees, a school month shall be construed as twenty school days, or four weeks of five days each and no teacher shall be required to teach school on Christmas day, the first day of January, the fourth day of July, the twenty-second day of February, the thirtieth day of May, the first Monday in September, election day in November, and the day appointed by the President of the United States or the Governor of this State as a day of Thanksgiving. And no deduction from the teacher's time or wages shall be made by reason of the fact that school day happens to be one of the days referred to in this section. And any contract made in violation of this section shall have no force or effect as against the teacher.

Section 1844. Every teacher shall have power to hold every pupil to a strict accountability in school for any disorderly conduct on the way to school, or during the intermission or recess; to suspend from school any pupil for good cause; Provided, That suspension shall be reported to the trustees as soon as practicable for their decision.

Section 1845. It sall be the duty of all teachers to endeavor to impress on the minds of their pupils the principles of morality, truth, justice and patriotism; to teach them to avoid idleness, profanity and falsehood, and to instruct them in the principles of a free government, and to train them up to a true comprehension of the rights, duties and dignity of American citizenship.

Section 1846. Any teacher who shall maltreat or abuse any pupil by administering any undue or severe punishment, shall be deemed guilty of a misdemeanor, and upon conviction thereof before any court of competent jurisdiction shall be fined in any sum not exceeding one hundred dollars.

Section 1847. No person is eligible to teach in any public school in this State, or to receive a certificate to teach, who has not attained the age of eighteen years.

Section 1848. In case of the dismissal of any teacher before the expiration of any written contract entered into between such teacher and board of trustees for alleged unfitness or incompetence, or violation of rules, the teacher may appeal to the county superintendent, and if the superintendent decides that the removal was made without good cause, the teacher so removed must be reinstated, and shall be entitled to compensation for the time lost during the pending of appeal.

Section 1849. Should any teacher employed by a board of school trustees for a specified time, leave the school before the expiration of such time, without the consent of the trustees in writing, said teacher shall be deemed guilty of unprofessional conduct, and the county superintendent is authorized, upon receiving notice of such fact, to suspend the certificate of such teacher for the period of six months. Should such teacher be the holder of a State certificate or life diploma, the county superintendent shall report the delinquency of the teacher to the State Board of Education, who are thereupon authorized to suspend said diploma for a period of one year.

ARTICLE VIII.
SCHOOLS.

Sec.	Sec.
1860. Common School defined.	1863. Sectarian publications forbidden.
1861. Course of study.	1864. School year.
1862. School hours.	

Section 1860. A common school is hereby defined to be one that is maintained at the public expense in each school district, and under the supervision of the board of trustees. Every common school not otherwise provided for by law, shall be open to the admission of all children between the ages of six and twenty-one years residing in the school district, and the board of trustees shall have the power to admit children not residing in the district, as hereinbefore provided.

Section 1861. All common schools shall be taught in the English language, and instruction shall be given in the following branches, viz: Reading, penmanship, orthography, written arithmetic, mental arithmetic, geography, English grammar, physiology and hygiene, with special reference to the effect of alcoholic stimulants and narcotics on the human system, history of the United States, civics of the United States and of Montana. Attention must be given during the entire school course to the cultivation of maners, to the laws of health, physical exercise, ventilation and temperature of the school room.

Section 1862. The school day shall be six hours in length, exclusive of an intermission at noon; but any board of trustees in any district having a population of five hundred or more may fix as the school day a less number of hours than six; Provided that it be not less than four hours, except in the lowest primary grades where the pupils may be dismissed after an attendance of two hours.
(Sec. 1862. Act approved March 8th, 1897.)

Section 1863. No publication of a sectarian, partisan or denominational character must be used or distributed in any school, or be made a part of any school library: nor must any sectarian or denominational doctrine be taught therein. Any school district, the officers of which knowingly allow any schools to be taught in violation of these provisions, forfeits all right to any State or county apportionment of school moneys; and upon satisfactory evidence of such violation the Superintendent of Public Instruction and county superintendent must withhold both State and county apportionments.

Section 1864. The school year shall begin on the first day of September and end on the thirty-first day of August.

ARTICLE IX.
PUPILS.

Section 1870. All pupils who may be attending public schools shall comply with the regulations established in pursuance of law for government of such schools; shall pursue the required course of study and shall submit to the authority of the teachers of such schools. Continued and wilful disobedience and open defiance of the authority of the teacher shall constitute good cause for expulsion from school. Any pupil who shall in any way cut, deface or otherwise injure any school house, furniture, fence or outbuilding thereof, or any book belonging to other pupils, or any books belonging to the district library, shall be liable to suspension and punishment, and the parent or guardian of such pupil shall be liable for damage on complaint of the teacher or any trustee, and upon proof of the same.

ARTICLE X.
DUTIES OF COUNTY TREASURER.

Section 1880. It shall be the duty of the county treasurer of each county:

First. To receive and hold all school moneys as special deposit and to keep a separate account of their disbursements to the several school districts which shall be entitled to receive them, according to the apportionment of the county superintendent of common schools.

Second. To notify the county superintendent of common schools of the amount of county school fund in the county treasury subject to apportionment, whenever required; and to inform said superintendent of the amount of school moneys belonging to any other fund subject to apportionment.

Third. To pay all warrants drawn on county or district school moneys, in accordance with the provisions of this act, whenever such warrants are countersigned by the district clerk and properly indorsed by the holders.

Fourth. To make annually during the month of October* in each year a financial report for the last school year and fiscal year ending with June** thirtieth to the county superintendent of common schools, in such form as may be required by him.

ARTICLE XI.
DUTIES OF COUNTY CLERK, CLERK OF DISTRICT COURT AND THE JUSTICES OF THE PEACE.

Sec.	Sec.
1890. Duty of county clerk.	1892 Duty of justice of the peace.
1891. Duty of clerk of district court.	1893. Penalty.

Section 1890. It shall be the duty of the county clerks of the several counties of the State to make a report to the county superintendent of common schools within their counties during the month of September in each year, of the school tax levied and the assessed valuation of the proper counties for that year.

Section 1891. It shall be the duty of the clerk of the district court at the close of every term thereof, to report to the county superintendent of the county in which said term shall have been held, whether or not any fines. and if any, what ones, were imposed by the court during the said term.

Section 1892. It shall be the duty of each justice of the peace of

---

* October should read September.
** June thirtieth should read August thirty-first.

each county to report to the county superintendent during the month oi September in each year, whether or not they have imposed and collected any fines during the preceding year, and if any, what ones, with the date at which the same were paid to the county treasurer.

Section 1893. All officers mentioned in sections 1890, 1891 and 1892 of this title, who shall fail or neglect to perform any of the duties required by this title, shall be deemed guilty of a misdemeanor, and upon conviction before any court having competent jurisdiction thereof, shall be fined in any sum not less than twenty dollars, and not more than one hundred dollars for each neglect; and such fine shall be paid into the county treasury for the benefit of common schools in said county.

ARTICLE XII.
TEACHERS' INSTITUTES.

Sec.
1900. Institutes in each county.
1901. Same.
1902. Sessions of Institute.

Sec.
1903. Notice. Teachers must attend.
1904. "Institute fund."
1905. Expenses of Institutes.

Section 1900. The county superintendent in every county in which there are five or more school districts, must hold one teachers' institute in each year; and every teacher employed in a public school in the county must attend the institute, and participate in its proceedings.

Section 1901. In any county where there are less than five school districts the county superintendent may, after conference with the Superintendent of Public Instruction, hold an institute.

Section 1902. Each session of the institute must continue not less than three nor more than ten days.
(Sec. 1902. Act approved March 8, 1897.)

Section 1903. When a teachers' institute has been appointed to be held for any county it may be the duty of the county superintendent to give written or printed notice to each teacher in the public schools of the county, and as far as possible to all others not engaged in teaching who are holders of teachers' certificate, at least thirty days before the opening of such institute of the time and place of holding it. Each teacher receiving such notice engaged in teaching a term of school which includes the time of holding such institute, may close school during such institute and attend the same upon permission of trustees of said district and may be paid by the school board of the district, regular wages as teacher for the time (not less than three days) he or she attended such instite, as certified by the county superintendent; Pro-

vided that no institute shall be held between the first day of June and the first day of September of any year.
(Sec. 1903. Act approved March 8, 1897.)

Section 1904. For the purpose of defraying the expenses of the institute mentioned in the preceding section of this act, there shall be an institute fund created as follows:

First. All moneys received from the issuance of teachers' certificates by the county superintendent.

Second. Moneys received from appropriations by boards of county commissioners: and every board of county commissioners in each county in which a teachers institute may be held is hereby authorized and directed to appropriate for said institue fund as follows:

Counties of the first class not less than $150.00 nor more than $250.00.

Counties of the second class not less than $100.00 nor more than $200.00.

Counties of the third class not less than $75 nor more than $125.

Counties of the fourth, fifth, sixth, seventh and eighth classes not less than $25 nor more than $100.
(Sec. 1904. Act approved March 8, 1897.)

Section 1905. The county superintendent must keep an accurate account of the actual expenses of the institute, with vouchers for the same, and present the bill to the county commissioners, who shall allow the same; Provided, that such amount shall not exceed that specified in the last preceding section of this title.

ARTICLE XIII.
EXAMINATIONS AND CERTIFICATES.

Sec.
1910. Examinations for certificates.
1911. Grades of certificates. Temporary certificate. Re-examination.
1912. Regulations cencerning certificates.

Sec.
1913. Charges.
1914. Revocation of certificate.
1915. Questions to be sealed.

Section 1910. The county superintendent shall hold public examinations of all persons over eighteen years of age, offering themselves as candidates for teachers of common schools, at the county seat, on the third Fridays in February, April, August and November of each year, and when necessary such examinations may be continued on the following day, at which time he shall examine them by a series of written or printed questions, according to the rules prescribed by the Superintendent of Public Instruction. If from the percentage of correct answers required by the rules, and other evidence disclosed by the examination, including particularly the superintendent's knowledge and information of the candidate's successful experience, the applicant is found to be a person of good moral character, to possess a knowledge and understanding, together with aptness to teach and govern, which shall enable such applicant to teach in the common schools of the State the various branches required by law, said superintendent shall grant to such applicant a certificate of qualification.

Section 1911. County Certificates shall be of four grades. The professional grade for a term of not less than four years, and the first grade certificate for a term of not less than three years, and the professional and first grade certificate shall be good and valid for as long as the holder thereof continues teaching and gives the county superintendent satisfactory evidence of progress and efficiency, the second grade certificate shall be valid for a term of two years, and the third grade certificate shall be valid for a term of one year, according to the ratio of correct answers of the applicant and other evidences of qualification appearing from the examination. No certificate shall be granted unless the applicant shall be found proficient in and qualified to teach the following branches of common English education: penmanship, orthography, reading, writing, arithmetic, mental arithmetic, geography, English grammar, physiology and hygiene, U. S. History, and theory and practice of teaching. In addition to the above, applicants for a second grade certificate shall pass a satisfactory examination in civics of the United Sttes and Montana, and physical geography; applicants for a first grade certificate shall pass an examination in civics of the United States and Montana, physical geography, American literture and elementary algebra; applicants for a professional grade certificate shall pass an examination in civics of the United States and Montana, physical geography, American literature, elementary algebra, physics and plane geometry. No person shall be employed as a teacher in high school or as the principal teacher of a school of more than two departments, who is not the holder of a professional County certificate or the holder of a life or State diploma, issued by the State Board of Education of the State of Montana, or who is not a graduate of some reputable University, College or Normal School. The percentages required to pass any branch shall, by a standing rule be prescribed by the superintendent of Public Instruction. In addition to these regular grades of certificates, the County Superintendent may grant a temporary certificate to teach until the next regular examination, to any person applying at any other time than at a regular examination, who can show satisfactory reasons for failing to attend such examination, subject to rules and regulations to be prescribed by the Superintendent of Public Instruction. Such temporary certificate shall not be granted more than once to the same person, Provided; that where a temporary certificate has been duly issued to any teacher, and that it is impossible, by reason of sickness or other unavoidable accident, for such teacher to attend the next regular examination, such teacher, upon due and sufficient proof certified to the County Superintendent, who shall certify the facts to the State Superintendent of Public Instruction, who may authorize the County Superintendent to issue a second permit or may require the teacher to take a private examination. The written answers of all candidates, for county certificates after being duly examined by the county superintendent, shall be kept by him during his term of office, and any candidate thinking an injustice has been done to him or her, by paying a fee of two dollars into the institute fund of the County and by notifying both County and State Superintendent of the same, shall have his or her paper re-examined by the Superintendent of Public Instruction. The County Superintendent shall upon receipt of such notice from said complaining candidate, transfer said paper to the Superintendent of Public Instruction. who shall re-examine the same, and if the answers warrant it shall instruct the County Superintendent to issue to such complaining candidate a county certificate of proper grade and the county superintendent shall carry out such instructions.

(Sec. 1911. Act approved March 4, 1837.)

Section 1912. No regular or temporary certificate to teach shall be issued to any person under the age of eighteen years, and no professional or first grade certificate shall be issued to any person who has not taught successfully twelve months; and a third grade certificate shall not be issued more than twice to the same person. Third and second grade certificates shall be valid only in the County where issued. A professional or first grade certificate shall be valid in any county in the State upon indorsement as hereinafter provided, and shall be renewed by the county superintendent upon the proper fee being paid to the institute fund as provided for in case of examination: Provided, that no professional or first grade certificate shall be renewed unless the applicant has taught at least ten months during the life of said certificate. Said professional or first grade certificate shall be renewed by the County Superintendent by his endorsement thereon, upon the payment of the same fee as is required by law for examinations; Pro-

vided further, that whenever application is made by a holder of any unexpired first grade, second grade, or third grade Montana certificate for examination for any higher grade certificates, and it shall be made to appear to the County Superintendent that such applicant has been engaged in teaching in any of the Public Schools of the State for a period of one year or more, the said applicant shall be entitled to be credited with the percentages on his or her last examination for said first, second or third grade certificate as the case may be, and shall not be required to be examined in any studies except the additional ones prescribed for such certificate, and such other studies that the applicant may not have secured the required percentage upon in previous examinations. Provided, further, that to excuse any candidate from taking the examination upon any branch of any grade he or she must have secured upon such branch at his or her last previous examination at least eighty per cent. No person shal be employed or permitted to teach in any of the public schools of the State who is not a holder of a lawful certificate of qualification to teach. Any contract made in violation of this Section shall be void; Provided, that the special certificate in penmanship, drawing, modern language and music shall be granted upon a request of a majority of the members of any district Board of Trustees. Such special certificate to be valid for three years, and shall entitle the holder to teach only such special branch or branches stated in said certificate, Provided, further, that if the attendance upon the aforesaid examination of teachers at the County seat shall work a great hardship to one or more teachers in the County, the county superintendent, upon application to the State Superintendent, may provide for such teacher or teachers to take the examination at some convenient place, and the county superintendent may appoint some suitable person to conduct such examination, under the rules and regulations prescribed by the State Superintendent of Public Instruction.
(Sec. 1912. Act approved March 4, 1897.)

Section 1913. Every applicant for a county certificate shall pay one dollar to the county superintendent, which shall be used by him in the support of teachers' institutes in the county.

Section 1914. The county superintendent is authorized and required to revoke and annul at any time a certificate granted by him or his predecessor for any cause which would have authorized or required him to refuse to grant it if known at the time it was granted, and for incompetency, immorality, intemperance, cruelty, crime against the State law, refusal to perform his duty, or general neglect of the business of the school. The revocation of the certificate shall terminate the employment of such teacher in the school in which he or she may at the time be employed, but the teacher must be paid up to the time of receiving notice of such revocation.

Section 1915. The questions prepared by the Superintendent of Public Instruction when received by the county superintendent shall not be opened or the seal thereof broken until the day of examination. And the county superintendent is prohibited from furnishing or giving to any person or persons any information concerning the questions prepared by the State Superintendent.

ARTICLE XIV.

COMPULSORY ATTENDANCE.

Sec.
1920. Compulsory attendance. Excuses.
1921. Penalty.
1922. Clerk must furnish list.

Sec.
1923. Prosecutions.
1924. Truant officer.
1925. Procedure.

Section 1920. Every parent, guardian or other person in the State of Montana, having control of any child or children between the ages of eight and fourteen years, shall be required to send such child or children to a public school, or private school taught by a competent instructor, for a period of at least twelve weeks in each year, six weeks of which time shall be consecutive; Provided, That such parent, guardian or other person having control of such child or children shall be excused from such duty by the school board of the district whenever it shall be shown to their satisfaction, subject to appeal as provided by law, that one of the following reasons exists therefore, to-wit:

First. That such child is taught at home by a competent instructor in such branches as are usually taught in the public schools.

Second. That such child has already acquired the branches of learning taught in the public schools.

Third. That such parent, guardian or other person is not able, by reason of poverty, to properly clothe such child.

Fourth. That such child is in such a physical or mental condition (as declared by a competent physician, if required by the board) to render such attendance inexpedient or impracticable.

Fifth. That there is no school taught the requisite length of time within two and one-half miles of the residence of such child by the nearest traveled road; Provided, that no child shall be refused admission to any public school on account of race or color.

Section 1921. Any parent, guardian or other person, failing to comply with the provisions of Section 1920 of this title, shall upon conviction, be deemed guilty of a misdemeanor, and fined in a sum not less than five nor more than twenty-five dollars for each offense; said action shall be prosecuted in the name of the State of Montana before any court of competent jurisdiction, and all fines so collected shall be paid into the county treasury and placed to the credit of the school fund of the district in which the offense occurs.

Section 1922. It shall be the duty of the district clerk of each school district not later than twenty days after the commencement of each school term to furnish the board of trustees with a list of names of all children between eight and fourteen years of age in attendance at school; and any district clerk failing to furnish such lists within the time specified herein shall be guilty of a misdemeanor and be liable to a fine of not less than five or more than twenty-five dollars for each offense; and such fine when collected shall be paid into the county treasury and placed to the credit of the school fund of the district in which the offense occurs.

Section 1923. It shall be the duty of the school trustees of the district to inquire into all cases of neglect of the duty prescribed in this title, and ascertain from the person neglecting, the reason, if any, therefor, and they shall forthwith proceed to secure the prosecution of any offense occurring under this title; and any trustee neglecting to secure such prosecution for such offense, within ten days after receiving the lists mentioned in Section 1922, unless the person so complained of shall be excused by the board of trustees for the reason hereinbefore stated, shall be deemed guilty of a misdemeanor and liable to a fine in the sum of not less than ten nor more than fifty dollars; and such fine when collected shall be paid into the county treasury and placed to the credit of the school fund of the district in which the offense occurs.

Section 1924. In every school district having a population of two thousand or more the board of trustees may appoint one person who shall be designated as "truant officer," whose duty it shall be, acting discreetly, to apprehend on view all children between eight and fourteen years of age, who are residents of the said district, who habitually frequent or loiter about public places, and have no lawful occupation, and place such children when so apprehended in the public school. And such officer shall report all cases of truancy to his respective board of trustees immediately. Upon the receipt of such information from such "truant officer," any member of the board of school trustees shall forthwith proceed to prosecute the person so offending as prescribed in Section 1920 of this title. Such officer shall be entitled to such compensation as shall be fixed by the board appointing him, which shall be paid out of the school fund.

Section 1925. If upon the trial of any offense as charged in Section 1923 it shall be made to appear to the satisfaction of the court or judge trying the same that such prosecution was malicious, then the costs in such case shall be adjudged against the complainant or person instituting such proceedings, and collected as fines in other cases.

ARTICLE XV.
CITY SUPERINTENDENT OF SCHOOLS.

Sec.	Sec.
1930. City superintendent of schools.	1932. Duties.
1931. Qualifications.	1933. Certain employment prohibited.

Section 1930. In every district having a population of five thousand and upwards, the board of trustees of such district may appoint a superintendent of schools, who shall be designated city superintendent of schools of the district and who shall hold his position at the pleasure of the board. He shall be paid a salary from the general school fund to be fixed by the board of trustees.

Section 1931. The person appointed to such position shall be the holder of a State certificate of the highest grade, issued in some state, or be a graduate of some reputable university, college or normal school, and shall have taught in public schools at least five years.

Section 1932. The superintendent shall perform such duties as the board of trustees shall prescribe.

Section 1933. No city superintendent shall engage in any work that will conflict with his duties as superintendent.

ARTICLE XVI.
SCHOOL FUNDS.

Sec.	Sec.
1940. State school fund. Taxation. Election.	1944. Transfer of road funds.
	1945. Proceeds of town lots.
1941. School tax; how collected.	1946. Building and furnishing fund.
1942. Apportionment.	1947. Warrants.
1943. Purposes for which money may be used.	1948. Transfer of funds. Election.

Section 1940. The principal of the State school fund shall remain irreducible and permanent. The said fund shall be derived from the following sources, to-wit: appropriations and donations by the State to this fund: donations and bequests by individuals to the state or com-

mon schools; the proceeds of land and other property which revert to
the state by escheat and forfeiture; the proceeds of all property granted
to the state, when the purpose of the grant is not specified or is uncertain; funds accumulated in the treasury of the state for the disbursement of which provision has not been made by law; the proceeds of
the sale of timber, stone, materials or other property from school lands
other than those granted for specific purposes, and all moneys other
than rental recovered from persons trespassing on said lands; five percentum of the proceeds of the sale of public lands lying within the
state which shall be sold by the United States subsequent to the admission of the state into the Union as approved by Section 15 of the
Enabling Act; the principal of all funds arising from the sale of lands
and other property which have been and may be hereafter granted to
the state for the support of common schools and such other funds as
may be provided by legislative enactment.

(Sec. 1940. Act approved March 8th, 1897.)

Section 1940a. In addition to the provisions for the support of the
common schools herein before provided, it shall be the duty of the
county commissioners of each county in the state to levy an annual tax,
which levy shall be made at the time and in the manner provided by
law for the levying of taxes for county purposes, and said levy shall
not be less than three mills on the dollar and not more than five mills
on a dollar of the assessed value of all taxable property real and personal, within the county which tax shall be collected by the county
treasurer at the same time and in the same manner as state and county
taxes are collected for the further support of common schools there
shall also be set apart by the county treasurer all moneys paid into the
county treasury arising from all fines for violations of law unless otherwise specified by law, such moneys shall be forthwith paid into the
county treasury by the officer receiving the same, and be added to the
yearly school fund raised by tax in each county and divided in the
same manner.

(Sec. 1940a. Act approved March 8th, 1897.)

Section 1940b. The board of trustees of any district may at any
time when in their judgment it is advisable submit to the qualified
electors of the district the question whether a tax not to exceed ten mills
on each dollar on the taxable property in the district shall be raised
to purchase lots and to furnish additional school facilities for said
district or for building one or more school houses, or for removing or
building additions to one already built, for the purchase of globes,
maps, charts, books of reference and other appliances or apparatus for

teaching or for any or all of these purposes. Such election shall be called by posting notices in three public places in the district for at least fifteen days before the election and by publishing for at least one time in some newspaper published in the county in which the said district is located a notice of such election provided that this shall apply only to districts containing a school board of more than three trustees and conducted as nearly as practicable according to the provisions herein made for holding annual school elections. The notice shall contain the time and place of holding the election the amount of moneys proposed to be raised and the purpose or purposes for which it is intended to be used. At such elections the ballot shall be in form as follows: "Shall a tax not to exceed.......... mills be raised to furnish additional school facilities for said district or for building a school house or for improving a school house or for building additions to one already built as the case may be.

Tax, Yes.

Tax, No.

The elector shall prepare his ballot by crossing out thereon parts of the ballot in such manner that the remaining part shall express his vote upon the question submitted. If a majority of the votes cast are "Tax, Yes" the officers of the election shall certify the fact to the assessor of the county who shall at once proceed to copy from the last assessment roll of the county assessor the list of property liable to taxation, situated in or owned by residents of his district and shall deliver the same to the board of trustees who shall allow him therefor out of the proceeds of said tax two dollars per day. The trustees shall upon receiving the roll, deduct ten percentum therefrom for anticipated delinquencies, and then by dividing the sum voted, together with the estimated cost of assessing and colleceting added thereto, by the remainder of the roll, ascertain the rate per centum required and the rate so ascertained (using the full cent on each one hundred dollars in the place of any fraction) shall be and is hereby levied and assessed to, on or against the persons or property named or described in said roll; and it shall be a lien on all such property until the tax is paid and said tax if not paid within the time limited within the next section for its payment shall be recovered by suit in the same manner and with the same costs as delinquent state and county taxes. The trustees upon receiving any assessment roll from the assessor shall give five days notice thereof by posting a notice in three public places in the district and shall sit for at least one day as a board of equalization at such time and place as shall have been named in said posted notices; and they shall have the same power as county boards of equalization to make any change in said assessment roll.

(Sec. 1940b. Act approved March 8th, 1897.)

Section 1941. As soon as the rate of taxation has been determined, as provided in the last preceding section, the trustees shall certify the same to the county clerk, who shall extend the same upon the general assessment roll of the county, and certify the same to the county treasurer, who shall proceed to collect the tax in the same manner and at the same time and with the same power and authority to enforce the payment of the same, as in the case of the State and county taxes. The county treasurer shall place any tax so collected to the credit of the district to which it belongs.

Section 1942. All school moneys apportioned by county superintendents of common schools shall be apportioned to the several districts in proportion to the number of school census children between six and twenty-one years of age, as shown by the returns of the district clerk for the next preceding school census; Provided, That Indian children who are not living under the guardianship of white persons, shall not be included in the apportionment list, unless the parents thereof are citizens of the United States, or have taken land under the allotment and severalty act of Congress, and have severed their tribal relations.

Section 1943. County school moneys may be used by the county superintendent and trustees for the various purposes as authorized and provided in this title, and for no other purpose, except that in any district, any surplus in the general school fund to the credit of said district, after providing for the expenses of not less than eight months school, may, on a vote of the qualified electors of said district, be used for the purposes of building and improvement.

If any school money shall be paid by the authority of the board of trustees for any purpose not authorized by this title, the trustees consenting to such payment shall be liable to the district for the repayment of such sum, and a suit to recover the same may be brought by the county attorney, or, if he shall refuse to bring the same, a suit may be brought by any tax-paying elector in the district.

Section 1944. It shall be the duty of the county treasurer in each county in this state, upon an order of the board of county commissioners, to transfer any and all sums of money raised by county road tax and apportioned to certain road districts, and shall have remained one year to the credit of any road district unused or unapportioned, to the credit of the particular school district or districts whose boundaries are coterminous, or nearly so, with those of the road district to whose credit said moneys were originally apportioned. A certificate of the road supervisor that such moneys are not needed for immediate use in building or repairing roads in his district, accompanied by the petition of ten residents of such district that such transfer be made, shall be made sufficient warrant for the county treasurer to make such transfer when approved by the board of county commissioners, and the official maps of the several road and school districts of the county shall determine the districts to which the transfers are to be made. Moneys so received to the credit of any particular school district may be applied by the trustees thereof to the payment of any outstanding district indebtedness, or, like other funds, to the ordinary expenses of the district.

Section 1945. All moneys arising from the sale of town lots under and by virtue of the several acts of the Legislative Assembly of the State of Montana relating to town sites, that are now or that hereafter may come into the hands of any clerk of the district court, or the corporate authorities of any city or town of this state, shall be paid into the county treasury of the county for the use and benefit of the common schools of the school district in which such city or town is situated, to be used as provided for in this title.

Section 1946. The county treasurers of the several counties of this State shall transfer all moneys so paid into said treasury, as provided for in Section 1945 of this title, or that may now be in such treasury, derived from said source, to the school fund of the school district in which town is situated, which shall be paid out on the order of the school trustees of such district, as provided for in Section 1947 of this title; and which said moneys shall be by said treasurer set apart as a special fund for the purpose of building and furnishing school houses, and shall be used for such purpose alone, unless otherwise ordered, as provided for in this title.

Section 1947. The school trustees of any school district are hereby authorized to draw warrants on said fund named in Sections 1945 and 1946 of this title, for the purpose of building and furnishing a school house in such place, in the town or city from the sale of lots out of which such funds arose, as they may designate, which said warrants or orders shall specify the fund on which the same are drawn and for what purpose drawn.

Section 1948. Said fund may be used for general school purposes, if a majority of the qualified electors of such district shall so elect, and upon the written request of any five of the qualified electors of such district, presented to the trustees for such purpose, said trustees shall order an election for such purpose in the manner provided in Section 1940, and the trustees shall prepare the form of the ballot used in such election, which election shall be conducted as other elections provided for in the several school districts under the general school laws of this State and when any warrant is so drawn on said fund for other purpose than the building and furnishing of a school house, said warrant shall specify that it was pursuant to an election held for such purpose.

ARTICLE XVII.
BONDS.

Sec.		Sec.	
1960.	How issued. Election. Limit.	1966.	Same. Redemption of bonds.
1961.	Same.	1967.	Redemption. Notice to bondholder.
1962.	Election. Ballots.	1968.	Duty of county treasurer.
1963.	Notice of sale of bonds.	1969.	Preparation of bonds.
1964.	School district liable on bonds.	1970.	Penalty.
1965.	Tax. Interest. Sinking fund.		

Section 1960. The board of school trustees of any school district within this state shall, whenever a majority of the school trustees so decide, submit to the electors of the district the question whether the board shall be authorized to issue coupon bonds to a certain amount, not to exceed three per cent of the taxable property in said district, and bearing a certain rate of interest not exceeding six per cent per annum, and payable and redeemable at a certain time, for the purpose of building and furnishing one or more school houses in said district and purchasing land necessary for the same. Should the trustees of any school district in which bonds have heretofore been issued to any amount desire to submit to the electors of the district the question as to whether additional bonds shall be issued, they may do so, but no such bonds shall be issued unless a majority of all the votes cast at any such election shall be cast in favor of such issue of additional bonds; and in no case shall the whole issue of bonds exceed the amount of three per cent of the taxable property within said school district.

Section 1961. The board of school trustees of any school district within Montana shall, whenever a majority of the school trustees so decide, submit to the electors of the district the question whether the board shall be authorized to issue coupon bonds to a certain amount not to exceed three (3) per cent of the taxable property in said district, provided, that nothing herein contained shall authorize the issuance of bonds to an amount exceeding two hundred and fifty-one thousand dollars in any one school district, and bearing a certain rate of interest not exceeding six per centum per annum and payable and redeemable at a certain time, for the purpose of building and furnishing one or more school houses in said district, and purchasing lands necessary for the same. Should the trustees in any school district in which bonds have been heretofore issued to any amount, desire to submit to the electors of the district the question as to whether additional bonds shall be issued, they may do so, but no such bonds shall be issued unless a majority of all the votes cast at any such election shall be cast in favor of such issue of additional bonds; and in no case shall the whole issues of bonds exceed in amount three per centum of the taxable property within said school district. This act shall not apply to an act entitled "An act to authorize the school trustees of the School District Number One, of Deer Lodge County, to issue additional bonds for certain purposes,'" approved February thirteenth, 1885.

Section 1962. Such election shall be held in the manner prescribed in Section 1940b of this title, but the ballots shall be in form as follows:

"Shall bonds be issued and sold to the amount of.............. thousand dollars, bearing............per cent interest, redeemable in ....years and payable in............years, for the purpose of purchasing a school lot, and building a school house thereon.

"Bonds, Yes;

"Bonds, No."

The elector shall prepare his ballot by crossing out thereon parts of the ballot in such a manner that the remaining part shall express his vote upon the question submitted. If a majority of the votes cast at such election are "Bonds, Yes," the board of school trustees shall issue such bonds in such form as the board may direct, and shall bear the signature of the chairman of the board of trustees, and shall be signed by the clerk as clerk of the said school district; and the coupons attached to the bonds shall be signed by the said chairman and said clerk. Provided, a lithographic or engraved fac simile of the signatures of the chairman and clerk may be affixed to the coupons only when so recited in the bonds. And each bond so issued shall be registered by the county treasurer in a book provided for that purpose, which shall show the number and amount of each bond, and the person to whom the same is issued. And the said bonds shall be sold by the said trustees as hereinafter provided.

Section 1963. The school trustees shall give notice by advertisement in some newspaper published in this state, for a period of not less than four weeks to the effect that the said school trustees will sell said bonds (briefly describing the same) and stating the time when, and place where, such sale will take place; Provided, That the said bonds shall not be sold for less than their par value, and that the said trustees are authorized to reject any bids, and to sell said bonds at private sale, if they deem it for the best interest of the district; and all moneys arising from the sale of said bonds shall be paid forthwith into the treasury of the county in which such district may be located, to the credit of said district and the same shall be immediately available for the purpose of building or providing the school houses authorized by this title; Provided, That no such bonds shall be delivered by the board of trustees unless the moneys therefor have been paid into the county treasury.

Section 1964. The faith of each school district is solemnly pledged for the payment of the interest and the redemption of the principal of the bonds which shall be issued under the provisions of this title. And for the purpose of enforcing the provisions of this title each school district shall be a body corporate, which may sue or be sued by, or in the name of, the board of school trustees of such district.

Section 1965. The school trustees of each district shall ascertain and levy annually, the tax necessary to pay the interest when it becomes due and a sinking fund to redeem the bonds at their maturity; and said tax shall become a lien upon the property in said school district, and be collected in the same manner as other taxes for school purposes.

Section 1966. The county commissioners, at the time of making the levy of taxes for county purposes, must levy a tax for that year upon the taxable property in such district, for the interest and redemption of said bonds, and such tax must not be less than sufficient to pay the interest of said bonds for that year, and such portion of the principal as is to become due during such year, and in any event must be high enough to raise, annually, for the first half of the term said bonds have to run, a sufficient sum to pay the interest thereon; and during the balance of the term, high enough to pay such annual interest, and to pay annually, a portion of the principal of said bonds equal to a sum produced by taking the whole amount of said bonds outstanding and dividing it by the number of years said bonds have to run; and all moneys so levied, when collected, must be paid into the county treasury to the credit of such district, kept in a separate fund and be used for the payment of principal and interest on said bonds, and for no other purpose.

1. Provided, that the board may with the surplus of such sinking fund, when the same shall be $1,000 or more, purchase, any of the outstanding bonds issued by the board. Such purchase shall be made

at the lowest price such bonds can be purchased at, but at no more than par value of such bonds; and whenever there shall be such a surplus of sinking fund amounting to the sum of $1,000, the board shall purchase therewith like bonds, on the same terms and conditions as hereinbefore specified.

2. If for any reason such bonds cannot be purchased as herein before specified, such sinking fund shall be invested by the Treasurer under the direction of the Board of Trustees, at such times as the board shall direct, in the interest-bearing bonds of the United States or of the State of Montana, and shall be purchased at the lowest market price. Interest accruing upon such bonds shall be invested in the same manner and for the same purpose as sinking fund.

Such bonds shall be held by the treasurer until the principal of any bonds issued by the board of trustees shall become due, and shall be sold at the highest market price, and the proceeds applied to the payment of the bonds; Provided further, that if at any time the Board shall deem it best, it shall be lawful for such bonds for the purpose of purchasing of the bonds issued by such board; but all such sales shall be at the highest market price, and the bonds of the board purchased with the proceeds of such sale shall be purchased at the lowest price they can be obtained for, and not above the par value of such bonds; Provided, further, that the bonds first maturing shall be purchased, if they can be purchased on terms as favorable to the board as others offered for sale to the said board.

All bonds of the said board purchased under the authority hereby given, or paid by the board, shall be forthwith cancelled as provided in the next succeeding section.

Section 1967. When the sum in said sinking fund shall equal or exceed the amount of any bond then due, the county treasurer shall give notice to each bondholder, if known to him, and shall post in his office a notice that he will, within thirty days from the date of such notice, redeem the bonds then payable, giving the numbers thereof, and preference shall be given to the oldest issue; and if at the expiration of the said thirty days the holder or holders of said bonds shall fail or neglect to present the same for payment, interest thereon shall cease; but the treasurer shall at all times thereafter be ready to redeem the same on presentation, and when any bonds shall be so purchased or redeemed, the county treasurer shall cancel all bonds so purchased and redeemed by writing across the face of such bond or bonds, in red' ink, the word "Redeemed" and the date of such redemption; Provided, That, whenever in the judgment of the board of school trustees and prior to the redemption of said bonds said board shall deem it advisable and for the best interests of the school districts to invest said sinking fund or any part thereof the board may by an order entered upon their minutes direct and require the county treasurer to invest said sinking fund or any part thereof in state or county bonds or warrants until such redeemable period.

Section 1968. The county treasurer shall pay out of any moneys belonging to a school district the interest upon any bonds issued under this title by such district when the same shall become due, upon the presentation at his office of the proper coupon, which shall show the amount due, and the number of the bond to which it belonged; and all coupons so paid shall be reported to the school trustees at their first meeting thereafter.

Section 1969. The school trustees of any district shall cause to be printed or lithographed, at the lowest rates, suitable bonds, with the coupons attached, when the same shall become necessary, and pay therefor out of any moneys in the county treasury to the credit of said school district.

Section 1970. If any of the school trustees of any district shall fail or refuse to pay into the proper county treasury the money arising from the sale of any bonds provided for by this title, they shall be deemed guilty of a felony, and upon conviction thereof, shall be punished by imprisonment in the State Penitentiary for a term of not less than one year nor more than ten years.

ARTICLE XVIII.
VACANCIES.

Sec.	Sec.
1980. Vacancy in school board.	1982. Trustee. How removed.
1981. Vacancy. Clerk.	

Section 1980. When any vacancy occurs in the office of trustee of any school district by death, resignation, failure to elect at the proper time, removal from the district or other causes, the fact of such vacancy shall be immediately certified to the county superintendent by the clerk of the school district, and the county superintendent shall immediately appoint in writing some competent person, who shall qualify and serve until the next annual school election. The county superintendents shall at the same time notify the clerk of the school district of every such appointment. Provided, That absence from the school district for sixty consecutive days shall constitute a vacancy in the office of trustee.

Section 1981. Should the office of the clerk of the school district become vacant, the board of school trustees shall immediately fill such vacancy by appointment, and the chairman of the board shall immediately notify the county superintendent of such appointment.

Section 1982. Any school trustee may be removed from office by a court of competent jurisdiction, as provided by law for removal of elective civil officers; Provided, however, that upon charges being preferred and good cause shown the board of county commissioners may suspend a trustee until such time as charges can be heard in the court having jurisdiction thereof.

ARTICLE XIX.
ARBOR DAY.

Sec.
1990. Arbor Day.
1991. Arbor Day exercises.

Sec.
1992. Same. Superintendent of Public Instruction.

Section 1990. The second Tuesday of May shall be known throughout the State as Arbor Day.

Section 1991. In order that the children in our public schools shall assist in the work of adorning the school grounds with trees, and to stimulate the minds of the children towards the benefits of the preservation and perpetuation of our forests and the growing of timber, it shall be the duty of the authorities in every public school district in this State to assemble the children in their charge on the above day in the school building or eleswhere, as they may deem proper, and to provide for and conduct under the general supervision of the city superintendent, county superintendent, teachers and trustees or other school authorities having the general charge and oversight of the public schools in each city or district, to have and hold such exercises as shall tend to encourage the planting, preservation and protection of trees and shrubs, and an acquaintance with the best methods to be adopted to accomplish such results.

Section 1992. The Superintendent of Public Instruction shall have power to prescribe from year to year a course of exercises and instructions in the subject hereinbefore mentioned, which shall be adopted and observed by the said public school authorities on Arbor Day.

Section 3280. For the purpose of advancing the interests of tree planting and arboriculture in this State, the second Tuesday in May is hereby designated as Arbor Day, and it is the duty of the Governor to annually make his proclamation setting apart that day for the planting of trees and for beautifying homes, cemeteries, highways, public grounds and landscapes, and the teachers in the public schools must on that day instruct the pupils as to the importance of tree planting and give practical lessons in landscape gardening.

Section 3282. The flower known as lewisia rediviva (bitter root) shall be the floral emblem of the State of Montana.

ARTICLE XX.
SCHOOL LIBRARIES.

Sec.	Sec.
2000. Library fund.	2003. Location and control of libraries.
2001. Same.	2004. Rules. Reports.
2002. Same.	2005. Selection of books.

Section 2000. A library fund is hereby created, and the board of school trustees must expend the library fund, together with such moneys as may be added thereto by donation, in the purchase of books for a school library, including books for supplementary work, and no warrant shall be drawn by the board of trustees against the library fund of any district unless such order is accompanied by an itemized bill, showing the books and the price of each, in payment of which the order is drawn.

Section 2001. Except in cities having a population of two thousand or more, the library fund shall consist of not less than five nor more than ten per cent of the county school fund annually apportioned in the district; Provided, that should such ten per cent exceed fifty dollars, fifty dollars only shall be apportioned to the district.

Section 2002. In cities having a population of two thousand or more the library fund shall consist of a sum not to exceed fifty dollars for every five hundred children or fraction thereof of three hundred or more, between the ages of six and twenty-one years annually taken from the general school fund of the county apportioned to such district.

Section 2003. Libraries shall be under the control of the board of trustees, and must be kept, when practicable, in the school houses.

Section 2004. The trustees shall be held accountable for the proper care and preservation of the library, and shall make all needful rules and regulations not provided for by the Superintendent of Public Instruction, and not inconsistent therewith; and they shall report annually to the county superintendent all library statistics which may be required by the blanks furnished for the purpose by the Superintendent of Public Instruction.

Section 2005. All books shall be selected from lists approved by the Superintendent of Public Instruction.

ARTICLE XXI.
MISCELLANEOUS.

Sec.		Sec.	
2020.	Gender.	2025.	School officers not to act as agents.
2021.	Fines and penalties.	2026.	Oath of office.
2022.	Insult to teacher.	2027.	Duty of county attorney.
2023.	Disturbance of school.	2028.	Penalties.
2024.	Printing and binding.		

Section 2020. Whenever the word "he" or "his" occurs in this title, referring either to the members of the board of trustees, county superintendent, teachers or other school officers, it shall be understood to mean also "she" or "her."

Section 2021. All fines and penalties, not otherwise provided for in this title, shall be collected by an action in any court of competent jurisdiction, and shall be paid into the county school fund immediately after collection.

Section 2022. Any parent, guardian or other person, who shall insult or abuse a teacher in the presence of the school, or anywhere on the school grounds or premises, shall be deemed guilty of a misdemeanor and liable to a fine of not less than ten dollars nor more than one hundred dollars.

Section 2023. Any person who shall willfully disturb any public school or any public school meeting, shall be guilty of a misdemeanor, and liable to a fine of not less than ten dollars nor more than one hundred dollars.

Section 2024. All printing or binding required under this title shall be executed in the form and manner and at a price not exceeding other county printing and shall be paid in like manner out of the general school fund.

Section 2025. Neither the Superintendent of Public Instruction, nor any person in his office, nor any county superintendent, nor school district officer, nor any officer or teacher connected with any public school, shall act as agent or solicitor for the sale of any school books, maps, charts, school library books, school furniture or apparatus or furnish any assistance to or receive any reward therefor from any author, publisher, bookseller or dealer, doing the same. Every person violating this section shall be guilty of a misdemeanor, and be liable to a fine of not less than fifty nor more than two hundred dollars for each offense, and shall be liable to removal from office therefor.

Section 2026. Any person elected or appointed to any office mentioned in this title shall, before entering upon the discharge of the duties thereof, take the oath of office. In case such officer has a written appointment or commission, his oath shall be endorsed thereon; otherwise it may be taken orally. In either case it may be sworn to before any officer authorized to administer oaths, and school officers are hereby authorized to administer all oaths relative to school business appertaining to their respective offices, without charge or fee.

Section 2027. The county attorney shall be the legal advisor of the county superintendent and all school trustees, and shall prosecute and defend all suits to which a district may be a party.

Section 2028. Any person who shall violate any provision of this title shall be deemed guilty of a misdemeanor (when not otherwise provided in this title) and upon conviction thereof shall be fined in a sum not less than twenty dollars nor more than two hundred dollars, or by imprisonment in the couty jail not less than five nor more than thirty days, or by both such fine and imprisonment.

CHAPTER VII.
DEAF AND DUMB ASYLUM.

Sec.
2330. Montana Deaf and Dumb Asylum.
2331. Objects.
2332. Control. Appointment of trustees.
2333. Meeting. Officers.
2334. Duty of board.
2335. Oath.
2336. Records.
2337. Compensation. Trustees and secretary.
2338. Superintendent. Control.
2339. Superintendent. Powers and duties.
2340. Exemption of employes.
2341. Officers not to be interested in contracts.
2342. Regulations concerning admittance.

Sec.
2343. Admittance of non-residents.
2344. Provision for pauper inmates.
2345. Duties of district clerk and superintendents of schools.
2346. Admittance of feeble minded persons.
2347. Expenditure of funds.
2348. State board of education. Powers.
2349. Term of school.
2350. Removal of trustee.
2351. By-Laws.
2352. Reports.
2353. Lands set apart for asylum.
2354. Deaf and dumb fund.

Section 2330. That the institution for the education of the deaf and dumb now located in the town of Boulder, Jefferson County, Montana, shall hereafter be known and designated as "The Montana Deaf and Dumb Asylum."

Section 2331. The object of said school shall be to teach the English language to all deaf and dumb children of the State, and to furnish all children who are debarred from the public schools by reason of deafness, dumbness, blindness or feeble-mindedness with at least an ordinary public school education in all customary branches, and to train them into mastery of such trades as shall enable them to become independent and self-sustaining citizens.

Increased facilities shall be furnished from time to time for the more thorough and successful training of those who may show a special aptness for acquiring said trades. This provision shall apply to the female as well as the male department of said school.

For the sake of economy and to the end that the aforesaid trades shall be practically taught to the pupils, it shall be the duty of the board of trustees to see that all the work necessary to be done for the school, such as carpentering, printing, painting, baking, sewing and the like shall, as soon as possible, be done by the pupils themselves, under the supervision of competent foremen or teachers, permanently or temporarily employed for that purpose.

Section 2332. The immediate control and management of said school shall be vested in a board of three (3) trustees, to be appointed by the State Board of Education, and to be divided into three classes, as follows:

Upon the taking effect of this act three (3) trustees shall be appointed, one of whom shall serve for the term of one (1) year, one of whom shall serve for two (2) years, and the remaining one shall serve for three (3) years from the date of their respective appointments; their successors, respectively, shall serve a term of three (3) years each; and in every case a trustee shall hold his office until his successor is duly appointed and qualified: Provided, that one member of said board shall be a resident of the town of Boulder, and the remaining members shall represent the state at large; and provided, further, that the superintendent or any other employe of said school shall not be a trustee thereof.

Section 2333. The said trustees shall meet in the town of Boulder within one month from the date of their appointment for the purpose of organization. They shall elect from their number a president and secretary, whose term of office shall be biennial. Two of the trustees shall at any time constitute a quorum for the transaction of business.

Section 2334. The said board of trustees shall hold a regular stated meeting on the second Tuesday of June, and every third month thereafter, also called meetings at the request of the superintendent or of any two of their own number.

At each regular meeting they shall carefully inspect the school under their charge, consult with the superintendent on all matters concerning the welfare of the school and transact all business arising by reason of the existence of said school.

They shall also appoint from their own number a committee of at least two (2) members, who shall serve in that capacity for such period as the board may designate, and whose duty it shall be to receive and examine all accounts appearing against said school for the preceding calendar month, and immediately to transmit all such as are approved to the State Board of Examiners for their re-examination and allowance; whereupon warrants on the State Treasury shall be issued for the full payment of said accounts.

To the end that said accounts may receive the necessary monthly attention, the aforesaid committee shall hold meetings on the second Tuesday of every month without necessary reference to the regular full meeting of the board of trustees.

All accounts shall specify clearly the nature of the claim or service and shall be countersigned by the superintendent and the chairman of said committee.

Section 2335. Each trustee, before entering upon the duties of his office shall take and subscribe an oath to support the Constitution of the United States and the Constitution of the State of Montana, and to faithfully discharge all the duties required of him by this act, which oath shall be filed in the office of the Secretary of the State.

Section 2336. The records of the secretary of the board shall at all times be open to the inspection of the trustees, the superintendent, the State Board of Education and the members of the Legislative Assembly.

Section 2337. The members of said board of trustees shall receive as compensation for their services, the sum of five dollars ($5.00) for each day employed, and ten cents (10c) per mile actually and necessarily traveled in attending meetings; provided, said compensation shall not exceed the total sum of one hundred and twenty-five dollars ($125.00) per annum for the individual trustee.

The secretary of the board shall receive as compensation for extra services required of him, the sum of one hundred dollars ($100.00) per annum, which sums shall be paid out of the State Treasury.

Section 2338. The said board of trustees shall have charge of the general interests of the school, and shall appoint for a term of two years at the time as superintendent a man of recognized Christian character who shall have acquired an easy and ready use of the "sign language," such as is commonly used by the educated deaf mutes; who shall have had at least three years actual experience in teaching the deaf; who shall be familiar with the methods used in general instruction of defective youths; who shall possess other qualifications necessary in their judgment to fit him for such office; Provided, that nothing herein shall be so contrued as to prevent the trustees from removing said superintendent by two-thirds (2-3) vote of the full board for incompetency, mismanagement or immorality. They shall fix the salary of said Superintendent, and he shall be eligible to re-election so long as they shall deem him worthy and fitted for said office.

Section 2339. The superintendent shall be the chief executive officer of the school and shall reside in the school or on the premises. He shall be purchasing agent for the trustees, and shall have charge under such regulations as they may prescribe, of the premises, property and pupils. He shall, with the approval and consent of the trustees, appoint and fix the compensation of the teachers and all subordinate officers and employes. He may at any time, if it seems best for the school and in the interest of harmony and good discipline, discharge any of them from service; Provided, that no teachers shall be discharged without the consent and approval of the trustees.

All such teachers, officers and other employes of said school shall be subordinate to the superintendent, and all orders to them or complaints from them shall pass through their hands. He shall see that all teachers, officers and other employes faithfully perform their respective duties, and he shall be held directly responsible to the trustees for economy, efficiency and success in all the internal work of the school.

He shall, before entering upon the duties of his office, take an oath to support the constitution of the United States and the constitution of Montana, and that he will discharge all the duties of his office with fidelity, to the best interests of the school under his care.

Section 2340. All persons employed in the school, while so employed shall be exempt from serving on juries or working on roads and highways, but not from paying road tax or property tax; and the certificate of the superintendent, under the official seal of the school, shall be sufficient evidence of such employment.

Section 2341. No trustee, superintendent or other officer or agent, appointed by virtue and under the provisions of this act shall have any direct or indirect interest, of personal benefit, in any contract or other agreement for building, repairing, furnishing or supplyling said school; and no drawbacks or secret discounts shall be given to or received by any such person on account of articles or material furnished to or labor done for said school.

Section 2342. The board of trustees, according to such rules and regulations as they may prescribe, on application shall admit into the school all deaf, dumb, blind and feeble-minded residing in the State of Montana, between the ages of six (6) and twenty-one (21) years, who are not unsound of mind or dangerously diseased in body, or of confirmed immorality or incapacitated for useful instruction by reason of physical disability. All pupils of said school shall be entitled to ten (10) years of attendance at said school, and upon special petition to the board by any pupil who has completed the course of ten years, which petition is approved by the superintendent, said pupil shall be allowed two additional years in the school; provided said grant of two additional years shall be conditioned upon the previous record of the petitioner as a pupil and as a moral character in the school, which record shall be considered by the board, who shall then judge as to the justice and utility of granting any extension of time to said petitioner; and provided further, that nothing in this section shall be so construed as to prevent suspension or expulsion of any pupil for insubordination or other good and sufficient cause.

Section 2343. Deaf and blind persons, not residents in the State of Montana, may be admitted into the privileges and advantages of the school, subject to all the personal qualifications prescribed in section 13 of this act, and not until the payment in advance of a sum of money, the amount of which shall be determined by careful estimate of the whole per capita cost of maintaining said school during the year immediately preceding the date of application by said non-resident persons; Provided, That no non-resident, deaf or blind person shall be admitted to the exclusion or detriment of any resident deaf or blind person.

Section 2344. In all cases where a person to be sent to said school is too poor to pay for necessary clothing and transportation, the judge of the District Court of the district where such person resides upon application of any relative or friend, or of any officer of the county where said person resides, shall, if he deem the person a proper subject, make an order to that effect, which shall be certified by the clerk of the court to the superintendent of said school, who shall then provide the necessary clothing and transportation at the expense of the county, and upon his rendering his proper accounts therefore quarter-annually, the county commissioners shall allow and pay the same out of the county treasury.

Section 2345. The school district clerk of each county in this State shall annually report to the county superintendent of schools the names, ages and postoffice addresses, and the names of parents or guardians, of every deaf or blind or feeble-minded person between the ages of five (5) and twenty-one (21) years residing in said school district, including all who are too deaf or blind to obtain an education in the public school.

The county superintendent of public schools shall, on or before the first day of August of each year, send a complete list of the names, ages and addresses of all such persons in said county to the superintendent of school for the defective.

Section 2346. All feeble-minded persons, resident in the State of Montana, and qualified after the general manner prescribed in Section 13 of this Act, shall be admitted into this school: Provided, That every such person shall be capable, in the judgment of the trustees, of at least some mental, moral or physical training, such as falls within the proper function of a school, as distinct from an asylum. To the end that the board of trustees may arrive at some definite method of judging such cases, they are hereby empowered to ascertain and establish certain tests, which tests shall be thoroughly and impartially applied to each case before final admission into the school, and it shall be the objects of said tests to ascertain in each case if there be any capacity for mental, moral or physical training; and provided further, that as soon as possible, in the judgment of the board of trustees, by and with the consent of the State Board of Education, a separate building and premises adjoining yet distinct from those of the deaf and blind, shall be provided for such feeble-minded persons, which building and premises shall be more especially adapted to the peculiar needs of said feeble-minded class of persons. The said feeble-minded department shall be under the general control and supervision of said board of trustees and superintendent, but the trustees, after consultation with the superintendent and at his request, may appoint an assistant superintendent, together with specially trained teachers and attendants, whenever in their judgment said feeble-minded department herein provided for shall seem to need such additional attention and supervision.

Section 2347. No moneys belonging to the "deaf and dumb fund" created by Sections 8 and 9 of the act of March 1, 1893, shall be otherwise expended than for the deaf and dumb department alone of this school; and no moneys belonging to any fund which may be hereafter created especially for the blind and feeble-minded department of this school shall be otherwise expended than for such department alone, is expressly designated in the act or acts creating such fund or funds.

Section 2348. The State Board of Education shall have power to receive, hold, manage and dispose of any and all real and personal property made over to them by purchase, gift, devise, bequest or otherwise, and the proceeds and interests thereof for the use and benefit of the school.

Section 2349. The regular term of school shall begin on the second Wednesday of September in each year and close on the second Wednesday of June following.

Section 2350. The State Board of Education shall have power to remove any trustee for inexcusable and repeated absence from meetings, or gross neglect of the duties prescribed in this act, or other good and sufficient reasons, and every such vacancy occurring by death, removal or otherwise, shall be filled in the manner prescribed in Section 3 of this act.

Section 2351. The board of trustees herein provided for shall, as soon as possible after their organization, and with the aid and advice of the superintendent, whom they shall have elected, formulate a set of by-laws for the wise regulation and government of the school, which by-laws shall be submitted to the State Board of Education for their approval and ratification. Said by-laws shall then be firmly and impartially enforced in the school, and any failure to comply with said by-laws shall submit the offender to a loss of employment or of the privileges and advantages of said school, at the option of the superintendent in consultation with the trustees.

Section 2352. On or before the first day of December, 1895, and annually thereafter, a report shall be made to the State Board of Education, which report shall include reports from the superintendent, the president of the board of trustees, and the visiting physician, and shall give complete and full information as follows, to-wit:

1st. The amount of moneys received and expended since the last report, in detail.

2nd. The estimated value of real estate and buildings, and the costs of all improvements, if any, made since the last report.

3rd. The number of pupils at any time in attendance since the last report, with names, ages and addresses, cause of deafness, etc.

4th. Health of the school, its sanitary condition, and any deaths or illness, if any, since the last report.

5th. The number of teachers, officers and employes in employment since the last report, with names, salaries, etc.

6th. All recommendations that may be deemed needful, and all other useful information touching any point of interest connected with said school at the time this report is made shall be set forth therein.

Ssection 2353. The lands heretofore granted by the government of the United States to the State of Montana, for the use and benefit of the deaf and dumb are hereby set apart and declared to be for the use in perpetuity of said school, and all funds arising from the sale or leasing of said lands or any part or portion thereof, shall be sacredly applied to the proper use and benefit thereof, and all donations, gifts, devises or grants which shall hereafter be made by any person or corporation to said school, shall rest in the State of Montana for the use and benefit thereof.

Section 2354. There is hereby created a fund to be known as the "deaf an dumb fund," in which all moneys for the use of said school shall be kept by the State Treasurer.

CHAPTER VIII.
AUTHORIZING THE STATE BOARD OF EDUCATION TO SELCE LANDS FOR EDUCATIONAL INSTITUTIONS.

Sec.	Sec.
3580. Selection of lands for educational Institutions.	3581. Certificate of selection.
	3582. Article not obligatory.

Section 3580. The State Board of Education is authorzied to select from the school lands and other public lands of the state suitable sites for the location of the State University, the Agricultural College and Experimental Station, the School of Mines, and the Normal School, within the limits prescribed in the Acts locating the said institutions respectively, which sites may include sufficient land for the proper use and maintenance of said institutions, and said lands when so selected, shall be, and they are hereby set apart and dedicated to and for the sole use and purpose of the said institutions.

Section 3581. It shall be the duty of said State Board of Education, when any selection shall be made by it under the authority of Section 1 of this act, to make a certificate of such selection, which certificate shall contain the date of such selection, a description of the lands selected, for what institution selected, and a reference to this act by its title, and the date of its approval, as the authority for its said action, and said certificate when so made shall be signed for said board by the President and Secretary thereof, and filed and recorded with the Clerk and Recorder of the county in which said lands are situated, and a copy thereof shall be filed with the State Board of Land Commissioners.

Section 3582. This Act shall not be construed as obligatory upon said State Board of Education to make such selection from the school or public lands of the State but it may in its discretion select such State or public lands or other lands as it may deem advisable for the best interests of said institutions.

CHAPTER IX.

TEXT BOOKS.

HOUSE BILL NO. 1.

An Act to create a Board of Text Book Commissioners for the purpose of establishing a uniform series of text-books for the public schools of Montana and to regulate the supply of the same, defining the duties and powers of said Board, and to appropriate for their expenses a sum of money therein named.

Section 1. The Superintendent of Public Instruction, the Attorney General, the President of the University, the President of the Agricultural College and three public school teachers actively engaged in public school work of the State, which said teachers shall be appointed by the Governor shall constitute a State Board of Text-book Commissioners, and who shall perform the duties hereinafter provided, and the Superintendent of Public Instruction shall be chairman of such board.

Section 2. The State Board of Text-book Commissioners shall meet at the office of the Superintendent of Public Instruction in the City of Helena, Montana, on the first Monday of May, 1897, for the purpose of selecting and adopting a uniform series of text-books for use in all public schools of the state. The said board shall appoint a secretary from one of their members and shall have power to formulate rules for its own government, and five members thereof shall constitute a quorum.

Section 3. Immediately upon the approval of this act, the superintendent of Public Instruction shall advertise for thirty (30) days in two (2) daily newspapers published in the State, giving notice that the State Board of Text-book Commissioners will meet, as herein aforesaid and receive sealed proposals up to 12 o'clock noon of said day for supplying the State of Montana with a uniform series of text-books for use in all the public schools of said state, for a term of six years from and after the first day of September, A. D. 1897, in the following branches, viz: Spelling, Reading, Suplementary Reading, Writing, Arithmetic, Geography, Grammar, Physiology and Hygiene, Civil Government, History of the United States, and in all other branches taught in the graded and common schools of the State. Said sealed proposals shall be addressed to the chairman of the State Board of Text-book Commissioners, Helena, Montana, and shall be endorsed "sealed proposals for supplying text-books for use in the State of Montana." Said proposals shall state the net wholesale price at which the publishers whose books may be adopted by the said text-book commission, will agree to deliver the same in the city of Chicago, F.

O. B. cars to merchants in Montana or school districts purchasing the same. They shall also state the exchange price for the new books adopted in exchange for the old books in the hands of the pupils that may be displaced, grade for grade and will further state a retail price at which the text-books so adopted shall be sold uniformly in at least one place in each county throughout the State. The publishers contracting and agreeing to supply books for use in the State of Montana under the provisions of this act, will cause to be prepared a special map and special supplement descriptive of Montana for the Geography adopted by the said Commission. They will also cause to be prepared a special supplement for Montana for the Civil Government adopted, which supplement shall contain not less than thirty pages. They shall further, agree to maintain the mechanical excellence of the books adopted by said Commission, at least equal to the samples submitted, in respect to binding, printing, quality of paper, and other essential features and the books shall be of the latest revised editions. The map and special descriptive Geography of Montana shall be revised every three years by the publisher.

Section 4. It shall be the duty of the said Board of Text-book Commissioners to meet at the time and place mentioned in said notice and open said sealed proposals in the presence of a quorum of said board, and in public, to select and adopt such text-books for use in the public schools as in their opinion will best subserve the educational interests of the State. The series of text-books so selected and adopted by the said Board of Text-book Commissioners shall be certified to by the Chairman and Secretary, and said certificate with a copy of all the books named therein shall be placed on file in the office of the State Superintendent of Public Instruction. Such certificate must contain a complete list of all the books adopted by the said board, giving the wholesale, retail and exchange prices for which each kind and grade will be furnished, as provided in the preceding section, and the name of the publisher agreeing to furnish same. The said books named in said certificate shall for a period of six (6) years from and after the first day of September, eighteen hundred and ninety-seven, be used in all the public schools of the state to the exclusion of all others.

Section 5. The said Board of Text-book Commissioners shall have power to make such contracts and agreements with publishers as they shall deem necessary for the best interests of the public schools of the State, and shall require of all publishers contracting and agreeing to furnish books adopted by the said Board of Text-book Commissioners bonds equal in amount to one-half of the value of the books to be furnished, and for the faithful performance of the conditions of the said contract; Provided, that the publishers contracting with the said Board of Text-book Commissioners shall agree to give the State of Montana the benefit of any reduction that may hereafter be made in the price of any book adopted by them and during the life of said contract; Provided, further, that the said Board of Text-book Commissioners may at their discretion, reject any and all proposals, if it is deemed by them to be to the interests of the State so to do, and they shall advertise for new proposals stating the time when such proposals will be received by them, not later however than thirty days from the rejection of the first proposal; Provided further, that the contract prices of such text books shall not exceed the lowest wholesale price charged for the same book in Chicago, F. O. B., to any State in the United States.

Section 6. The contract with the publishers shall take effect only when the publishers of the books adopted by said Text-book Commission shall have filed with the Secretary of State, their bond, with at least sufficient sureties, to be approved by the Governor in such sum as shall be determined by the said Board of Text-book Commissioners; conditioned, that they shall comply with the terms of their proposal to the State and such further conditions as may be agreed upon between the said Board of Text-book Commissioners and the publishers contracting with the State.

Section 7. In case the publishers of the books adopted by said Board of Text-book Commissioners shall not, on or before the first day of July, A. D. eighteen hundred and ninety-seven, have filed with the Secretary of State their bond as hereinbefore provided, or in case they shall not on or before the first day of July, A. D. eighteen hundred and ninety-eight, have performed all the obligations of their bonds, with respect to the exchange and introduction of books, and the preparation and supply of the special map and special descriptive matter for the Geography so adopted, or the special supplement for the Civil Government, or in case they shall at any time thereafter violate or fail to perform any of the conditions specified in their bond as hereinbefore provided, and shall fail within a reasonable time after due notice shall have been given them by the State Superintendent of Public Instruction to make good their guarantee in any respect in which they may have failed, then this adoption shall become null and void. The said text-books adopted by the said Text-book Commission under this Act, and upon compliance by the publishers of the conditions aforesaid shall continue in use for the period of six (6) years from the first day of September, eighteen hundred and ninety-seven, to the exclusion of all others, and until otherwise provided by Statute.

Section 8. Whenever the publishers of the books adopted under the provision of this bill shall have filed their bond, as hereinbefore provided for, it shall be the duty of the State Superintendent of Public Instruction to cause all prices of the text-books as guaranteed by the publishers to be properly printed and distributed through the county superintendents to the trustees of all school districts in the State who shall cause the same to be kept constantly posted in a conspicuous place in each school room in their district ,and it shall be the duty of the several county superintendents to keep themselves informed as to whether such prices are actually maintained by the said publishers.

Section 9. Any school officer, teacher or trustee who shall use or provide for the use in any of the public schools of the State, of text-books other than those adopted by the said State Board of Text-book Commissioners shall be deemed guilty of a misdemeanor.

Section 10. All County Superintendents and school officers are charged with the execution of this law and the County School Superintendents shall require the trustees of the several school districts, or the clerks thereof, to report annually whether or not the authorized text-books are used in their schools.

Section 11. Upon the petition of ten (10) legal voters of any school district other than in incorporated cities, and upon petition of one hundred (100) legal voters in incorporated cities, towns and villages filed with the Board of Trustees or Board of Education, as the case may be, fifteen days preceding a regular annual election of trustees or members of the Board of Education, it shall be the duty of the Board of Education or the School Trustees, as the case may be, to notify the voters of such school district that an election "for" or "against" free text-books will be held at next ensuing election for members of the Board of Education or School Trustees, and the ballots to such effect shall be received and canvassed at such election; and if a majority of all the votes cast in the district shall be found by such vote to be in favor of free text-books, it shall be the duty of the trustees or Board of Education, as the case may be, to purchase at the expense of such school district all the text-books required for the use of the pupils attending school in such school district; and such text-books shall be loaned to the pupils of said public school, free of charge, subject to such rules and regulations as to care and custody as the Board of Education or School Trustees may prescribe; Provided, that pupils may purchase at cost any of the text-books so furnished, when desired by them.

Section 12. That for the purpose of raising money to pay for school books which may be furnished to pupils free by any district adopting free text books a special levy on the taxable property of said district shall be made by the County Commissioners of the County on estimates furnished by the school trustees of the district, if the money received from the district from the general fund be insufficient, and said levy shall be made within thirty days from, and after the adoption of said free text-books in any district that has by majority vote adopted the same and when so made the tax levied shall be collected in the same manner as other taxes are collected.

Section 13. The said Board of Text-book Commissioners provided for by this act, except the State Superintendent of Public Instruction, the Attorney General, President of Agricultural College, President of University of Montana, shall receive the sum of six dollars per diem for each day necessarily engaged in transacting business, and while in session, and ten cents per mile each way for each mile necessarily traveled, and there is hereby appropriated the sum of one thousand dollars ($1,000), or so much thereof as may be necessary to carry out the provisions of this Act.

Section 14. All acts and parts of acts in conflict with the provisions of this Act, be and the same are hereby repealed.

Section 15. This Act shall take effect and be in force from and after its passage and approval.

(Approved March 1st, 1897.)

SENATE BILL NO. 1.
CHAPTER X.
UNIVERSITY BOND BILL.

An Act to provide for the erection, completion, furnishing and equipment of buildings for the University of Montana.

Section 1. The State Board of Land Commissioners of the State of Montana is hereby authorized to issue bonds to the amount of one hundred thousand dollars ($100,000.00), the minimum denomination of which shall be fifty dollars ($50.00) and the maximum denomination shall be one thousand dollars ($1,000.00) each; said bonds to be known as the State University Bonds, which shall bear date of July first, 1897, to become due thirty (30) years after date and payable after twenty (20) years after date thereof; said bonds shall bear interest at the rate of not more than six (6) per cent per annum payable semi-annually on the first day of January and July of each year at the office of the State Treasurer of the State of Montana; said bonds shall run from the State Board of Land Commissioners of the State of Montana to bearer, and shall be signed by the State Board of Land Commissioners and countersigned by the Secretary of State, who shall attach his seal thereto.

Section 2. The bonds provided for in the first section of this Act shall be issued and sold as soon as possible after the passage of this Act.

Section 3. All funds realized from the sales of licenses to cut trees, leasing of said lands or from the profits arising from the permanent fund to be created, as provided for by Section 14 of an Act of Congress, approved February 22, 1889, entitled "An Act to provide for the division of Dakota into two States, and to enable the people of North Dakota, South Dakota, Montana and Washington to form constitutions and State Governments ,and to be admitted into the Union on an equal footing with the Original States and to make donations of public lands to such States" (said land being forty-six thousand and eighty (46080) acres) granted to the Territory of Montana by the Act of February 18, 1881, and vested in the State of Montana by the act of February 22, 1889) for the establishment and maintenance of a University; are hereby pledged as security for the payment of the principal and interest of the bonds authorized by this Act, and all revenue or profits derived from the said lands or said permanent fund to be created, or any of them, whether on account of lease, sales of licenses to cut trees, or otherwise, are hereby set apart and shall constitute a fund for the payment as hereinafter provided of the principal and interest of the said bonds, which bonds shall be a first lien on said University Bond Fund.

Section 4. It shall be the duty of the State Treasurer to keep all moneys derived from the University lands hereinbefore mentioned in a separate fund, to be known and designated as the University Bond Fund and out of the moneys of such fund, he shall pay after approval by the State Board of Examiners:

First: The cost and expenses of issuing of the bonds herein provided for—

Second: The interest on the bonds herein authorized when due, and,

Third: When bonds shall become payable, he shall call in and pay them as rapidly as the moneys in such fund will permit after providing for the interest. That in the event there shall not be sufficient funds in the University Bond Fund to pay the interest when due, the State Board of Examiners shall, by an order entered upon their minutes cause warrants to be issued on the University Bond Fund for the amount of the interest due, and the warrants so issued shall draw interest at the rate of six (6) per cent per annum, and said warrants shall be paid by the Treasurer as soon as sufficient funds accumulate in said fund to pay the same ,and by reason of the delivery of the said warrants to the holders of the said bonds in satisfaction of the accrued interest, there shall be no default in the payment of the interest.

Section 5. It shall be the duty of the State Treasurer to give notice, by advertising for not less than two (2) weeks daily in one newspaper, published in the City of Helena, Montana, and in one newspaper published in the City of New York. that he will on April fifth, 1897, sell one hundred thousand dollars ($100,000.00) of the bonds herein authorized and will receive bids therefor and said bonds shall on said day be by him sold to the highest bidder: Provided, that the State Board of Education shall open all bids and shall have the right to reject any or all bids. If no bids are then received and accepted said bonds may then be sold afterwards at private sale, provided however, that none of the said bonds shall at any time be sold at less than par.

Section 6. The moneys derived from the sale of the said bonds shall be used to erect, furnish and equip buildings for the use and benefit of the University of Montana at the City of Missoula in said State, and shall by the State Treasurer be paid out on the warrants of the building commission of said University as hereafter provided.

Section 7. There is hereby created a building commission to be composed of five persons to be appointed by the Governor of the State, no more than two of whom shall be of the same political party and all residents of the City of Missoula, who shall serve without compensation, whose duty it shall be to contract for the erection and furnishing of suitable buildings for the use and benefit of the University of Montana, the said commission shall have charge and supervision over the construction of said buildings and all things pertaining thereto; and shall have authority from time to time to draw their warrants on the Treasurer of the State of Montana for such sum or sums as may be due any contractor or employe engaged in and about the erection of the said buildings which warrants shall be paid by the said State Treasurer out of any funds in his hands arising from the sale of bonds provided for in this act. Said Building Commission is hereby authorized to employ an architect and such other assistants as it may deem necessary in preparing the plans, specifications and superintending the construction of said buildings and the expense thereof shall be paid out of the funds as hereinbefore provided for the erection of said buildings, provided that all architects, superintendents and contractors shall be citizens of the State of Montana. Said Commission shall make report from time to time, to the stated meetings of the State Board of Education, of the progress of said work and the expenditures therefor.

Section 8. The State of Montana shall in no wise be held liable for the payment of the bonds herein authorized or interest thereon.

(Approved March 4th, 1897.)

SENATE BILL NO. 74.
CHAPTER XI.
SCHOOL OF MINES BOND BILL.

An Act authorizing the issuance of bonds to provide for the payment of outstanding warrants and for the erection and completion of a building for the school of mines at the City of Butte and providing for the payment of interest thereon, and repealing sections 1584, 1600 and 1601 of the Political Code of Montana.

Section 1. The Board of School of Mines Commissioners and the State Board of Land Commissioners of the State of Montana are hereby authorized to issue and dispose of bonds for the purpose of erecting a building to be known as the "School of Mines Building" to be located in the City of Butte, Montana, under the following conditions and restrictions, to-wit:

First. The aggregate amount of bonds authorized by this Act shall not exceed the sum of One Hundred and Twenty Thousand Dollars ($120,000).

Second. The denomination of each bond shall be one hundred dollars, or any multiple thereof, but the maximum amount of any bond shall not exceed the sum of One Thousand Dollars.

Third. The term of said bonds shall not exceed thirty years from their date, and they shall be payable at any time after fifteen years from their date at the option of the issuers.

Fourth. The bonds may bear any rate of interest not in excess of six per centum per annum, and the interest may be payable semi-annually.

Fifth. The principal and interest shall be payable at such place and in such manner as is designated in the bond.

Sixth. The Board of School of Mines Commissioners and the State Board of Land Commissioners shall prescribe the form of the bond, the bonds shall bear upon their face the words "School of Mines Building Bond of the State of Montana" and they shall be signed by the members of the Board of School of Mines Commissioners and the State Board of Land Commissioners and shall be countersigned by the Secretary and Treasurer of the State and the seal of the state, shall be affixed to each bond, and the bonds shall be registered in the office of the State Treasurer.

Seventh. The coupons representing the interest on the bonds shall be signed by the State Treasurer, or an engraved or lithographic facsimile of the signature of the Treasurer may be affixed thereto provided it is so authorized in the bond.

Section 2. The bonds provided for in this act shall be disposed of by the Board of School of Mines Commissioners and the State Board of Land Commissioners in such a manner as they shall deem it for the best interests of the State, provided, that no bond shall be disposed of for less than its par value.

Section 3. To provide for the payment of the interest and principal of the bonds authorized by this act, there is hereby created a special fund to be known as "The School of Mines Building Interest and Sinking Fund," into which shall be paid all sums of money realized from sales of lands, licenses to cut trees, leasing of lands, profits of any and all other sources by reason of the grants of lands by Congress to the State of Montana for the establishment and maintenance of a school of mines, as provided by sections 12 and 17 of an act of the United States Congress entitled "An Act to provide for the division of Dakota into two states, and to enable the people of North Dakota, South Dakota, Montana and Washington to form constitutions and State Governments, and to be admitted into the Union on an equal footing with the original States, and to make donations of public lands to such states," approved February 22nd, 1889, and from said "School of Mines Building Interest and Sinking Fund" there shall, as the same become due and payable, be paid the interest on said bonds; and it is further provided, that it is the duty of the "State Board of Land Commissioners" whenever there are any funds in the said "School of Mines Building Interest and Sinking Fund" over and above the sum of twenty-five hundred dollars in excess of the amount required to pay the yearly interest on said bonds, to invest such excess funds in the manner set forth and provided in section 4 of this act, and the amount so invested shall constitute a "permanent fund" to pay the principal of the said bonds; but all interest or profit derived from the investment shall be paid into the said "School of Mines Building Interest and Sinking Fund" and the principal and interest of the said bonds shall be a first lien upon said funds; and all the lands granted and belonging to the State, for the purpose of establishing and maintaining a School of Mines.

Section 4. The State Board of Land Commissioners are hereby authorized and directed to create a "permanent fund" for the payment of the bonds authorized by this act, from the following revenues, to-wit: Whenever the revenues in any year are sufficient to pay the interest on the said bonds and there shall be in excess thereof the sum of twenty-five hundred dollars, then any and all funds over and above the said sum of twenty-five hundred dollars shall be invested for the benefit of the "School of Mines Building Interest and Sinking Fund" as follows, to-wit:

First. In the bonds authorized by this act, provided they can be purchased at a cost not exceeding their par value and accrued interest.

Second. In any legally issued bonds of any county, school district, city or town of the State of Montana, provided they can be purchased at a cost not exceeding their par value and interest.

Third. In any legally issued General Fund Warrants of the State of Montana, or any legally issued warrants of county, city or town of the State of Montana, provided they can be purchased at a cost not exceeding their par value and accrued interest; and the said Board of Land Commissioners are hereby granted discretionary power in the selection and purchase of the securities hereinbefore described, as to the amount of each they shall purchase and conditions of general credit affecting the same.

Section 5. It is hereby provided and set forth, that in the event the State of Montana shall at any time provide and pay the interest, or any part thereof, on the bonds authorized by this act, from the general fund of the state, or by any special appropriation made or tax levied therefor, then for any and all interest so paid, the State shall be reimbursed from the said "School of Mines Building Interest and Sinking Fund", by the payment of the amount so paid or due, whenever there is sufficient money in said "School of Mines Building Interest and Sinking Fund" to pay the same.

Section 6. The State Treasurer is hereby designated as the custodian of the funds provided by this act and he shall pay all warrants properly drawn by the "Board of School of Mines Commissioners" save and excepting as to the interest on the bonds, which he shall pay as the same becomes due and charge the amount thereof to the "School of Mines Building Interest and Sinking Fund" hereinbefore created.

Section 7. All moneys received from the sale of the bonds authorized by this act shall be paid to the State Treasurer, and shall constitute a special fund for the erection of the "School of Mines Building, and shall be disbursed by the State Treasurer on warrants properly drawn by the "Board of School of Mines Commissioners" and including all warrants heretofore drawn by the "Board of School of Mines Commissioners" and registered prior to the passage of this act.

Section 8. Whenever any of the bonds authorized by this Act shall become due and payable, and there is sufficient funds to pay the same, they shall be called in and paid in the order of their issuance, beginning with the lowest number.

Section 9. The cost and expenses of issuing the bonds hereinbefore authorized may be paid out of the proceeds thereof, or be chargable to the expense of the construction of the building.

Section 10. In the event there shall not at any time be sufficient money in the "School of Mines Building Interest and Sinking Fund" to pay the interest when due, the State Board of Land Commissioners and the Board of School of Mines Commissioners shall, by an order entered on their minutes or record books, cause warrants to be issued on the said "School of Mines Building Interest and Sinking Fund" for the amount of interest due, and the warrants so issued shall be registered in the office of the Treasurer of the State, and shall bear interest at the rate of six per centum per annum, and said warrants shall be paid by the State Treasurer whenever there is sufficient money accumulated in said fund to pay the same, and by reason of the delivery of said warrants to the holders of said bonds and the surrender of the interest coupons, there shall be no default in the payment of interest.

Section 11. Nothing in this act shall be so construed as to in any wise hold the State of Montana liable for the payment of the bonds herein authorized, except as to the lien heretofore created against the lands and funds granted for the purpose of establishing and maintaining the School of Mines and which lien shall not be abridged, annulled or set aside until the bonds authorized by this act shall have been fully paid, together with the interest thereon and the Governor is hereby specially authorized and empowered to use all lawful means to enforce the provisions of this act.

Section 12. Sections 1584, 1600 and 1601 of the Political Code of the State of Montana and all acts and parts of acts in conflict with this act are hereby repealed.

Section 13. There is hereby appropriated from the proceeds of the sale of bonds authorized by this act the sum of one hundred and twenty thousand dollars ($120,000) for the fiscal year ending December the first, 1897.

Section 14. This act shall be in full force and effect from and after its passage and approval by the Governor.

(Approved March 8th, 1897.)

SENATE BILL NO. 69.
CHAPTER XII.
DEAF AND DUMB ASYLUM BOND BILL.

An Act authorizing the issuance of bonds to provide for the payment of all outstanding Deaf and Dumb Asylum Building Warrants, to complete the building now in course of construction at the town of Boulder, County of Jefferson, State of Montana, and to erect certain buildings, make certain improvements on the grounds of said Deaf and Dumb Asylum at said place, and to create a sinking fund to redeem said bonds and to repeal all conflicting laws.

Section 1. The state board of education and the state board of land commissioners of the State of Montana are hereby authorized to issue and dispose of bonds for the purpose of providing for the payment of all outstanding Deaf and Dumb Asylum Building Warrants, to complete the building now in course of construction at the town of Boulder, County of Jefferson, State of Montana ,and to erect certain improvements on the grounds of said Deaf and Dumb Asylum at said place, under the following conditions and restrictions, to-wit:

First: The aggregate amount of bonds authorized by this act shall not exceed the sum of sixty-five thousand dollars.

Second: The denomination of each bond shall be one hundred dollars, or any multiple thereof, but the maximum amount of any bond shall not exceed the sum of one thousand dollars.

Third: The terms of said bonds shall not exceed thirty years from their date, and they shall be payable at any time after fifteen years from their date at the option of the issuers.

Fourth: The bonds may bear any rate of interest not in excess of six per centum per annum and the interest may be payable semi-annually.

Fifth: The principal and interest shall be payable at such place and in such maner as is designated in the bond.

Sixth: The State Board of Education and the State Board of Land Commissioners shall prescribe the form of the bonds. The bonds shall bear upon their face the words "Deaf and Dumb Asylum Bond of the State of Montana," and they shall be signed by the members of the State Board of Education and the State Board of Land Commissioners and shall be countersigned by the Secretary and Treasurer of the State, and the seal of the State shall be affixed to each bond and the bonds shall be registered in the office of the State Treasurer.

Seventh: The coupons representing the interest on the bonds shall be signed by the State Treasurer, or an engraved or lithographic facsimile of the signature of the Treasurer may be affixed thereto, provided, it is so authorized in the bond.

Section 2. The bonds provided for in this act shall be disposed of by the State Board of Education and the State Board of Land Commissioners, in such manner as they shall deem it for the best interests of the State, provided, that no bond shall be disposed of for less than its par value.

Section 3. To provide for the payment of the principal and interest of the bonds authorized by this Act, there is hereby created a special fund to be known as "The Deaf and Dumb Asylum Interest and Sinking Fund," into which shall be paid all sums of money realized from sales of lands, licenses to cut trees, leasing of lands, profits of any and all other sources by reason of the grants of lands by Congress to the State of Montana for the establishment of a Deaf and Dumb Asylum, as provided by Section 12 and 17 of an Act of the United States Congress entitled "An Act to provide for the division of Dakota into two states and to enable the people of North Dakota, South Dakota, Montana and Washington to form constitutions and state governments, and to be admitted into the Union on an equal footing with the original states, and to make donations of public lands to such states, approved February 22, 1889, and from said Deaf and Dumb Asylum interest and sinking fund there shall as the same becomes due and payable, be paid the interest on the said bonds; and it is further provided that it is the duty of the State Board of Land Commissioners whenever there are any funds in the said "Deaf and Dumb Asylum interest and sinking fund," over and above the sum of twenty-five hundred dollars in excess of the amount required to pay the yearly interest on said bonds, to invest such excess funds in the manner set forth and provided in section 4 of this Act, and the amount so invested shall constitute a permanent fund, to pay the principal of said bonds; but all interest or profit derived from the investment shall be paid into the said "Deaf and Dumb Asylum Interest and Sinking Fund" and the principal and interest of the said bonds shall be a first lien upon said funds, and all lands granted and belonging to the State, for the establishment of a Deaf and Dumb Asylum.

Section 4. The State Board of Land Commissioners are hereby authorized and directed to create a permanent fund for the payment of the principal of the bonds authorized by this Act, from the following revenues, to-wit:

Whenever the revenues of any year are sufficient to pay the interest on said bonds and there shall be an excess thereof the sum of twenty-five hundred dollars, then any and all funds over and above the said sum of twenty-five hundred dollars shall be invested for the benefit of the "Deaf and Dumb Asylum Interest and Sinking Fund" as follows, to-wit:

First. In the bonds authorized by this Act, provided they can be purchased at a cost not exceeding their par value and accrued interest.

Second. In any legally issued bonds of any county, school district, city or town of the State of Montana, provided, they can be purchased at a cost not exceeding their par value and accrued interest; and the said State Board of Land Commissioners are hereby granted discretionary power in the selection and purchase of the securities hereinbefore described, as to the amount of each they shall purchase and conditions of general credit affecting the same.

Section 5. It is hereby provided and set forth that in the event the State of Montana shall at any time provide and pay the interest or any part thereof on the bonds authorized by this Act, from the general fund of the state, or by any special appropriation made or tax levied therefor, then for any and all interest so paid, the State shall be reimbursed from the said "Deaf and Dumb Asylum Interest and Sinking Fund" by the payment of the amount so paid or due, whenever there is sufficient money in said "Deaf and Dumb Asylum Interest and Sinking Fund to pay the same.

Section 6. The State Treasurer is hereby designated as the custodian of the funds provided by this Act, and he shall pay all warrants properly drawn by the State Board of Examiners save and excepting as to the interest on the bonds, which he shall pay as the same becomes due and charge the amount thereof to the "Deaf and Dumb Asylum Interest and Sinking Fund" hereinbefore created.

Section 7. The moneys received from the sale of the bonds authorized by this Act, shall be paid to the State Treasurer and shall constitute a special fund for the following purposes:

First: Fifty thousand dollars thereof or so much as may be necessary to redeem and pay all legal and outstanding warrants drawn on the "Deaf and Dumb Asylum Building Fund," with accrued interest, and to complete and furnish the Deaf and Dumb Asylum Building at Boulder, Montana, in accordance with the plans and specifications of the existing contracts.

Second: Thirteen thousand dollars ($13,000) thereof, or so much as may be necessary to erect and furnish a suitable and separate building on the grounds of the Deaf and Dumb Asylum at Boulder, Montana, for the temporary use and care of the feeble-minded.

Third: Two thousand dollars ($2,000.00) thereof, or so much as may be necessary to grade, fence and otherwise improve the grounds of the Deaf and Dumb Asylum at Boulder, Montana. In making contracts for the erection of said buildings and in making payments therefor, and in all things pertaining thereto, the provisions of Article III, Sections 2361 to 2370 of the Political Code of Montana inclusive, shall control so far as practicable. The local board of trustees with the approval of the State Board of Examiners are authorized and empowered to change the amounts above mentioned in such manner as shall best meet the purposes of this Act.

Section 8. Whenever any of the bonds authorized by this Act shall become due and payable, and there is sufficient funds to pay the same, they shall be called in and paid in the order of their issuance beginning with the lowest number.

Section 9. The cost and expense of issuing the bonds hereinbefore authorized may be paid out of the proceeds thereof, or be chargeable to the expense of the construction of the buildings.

Section 10. In the event there shall not at any time be sufficient money in the "Deaf and Dumb Asylum Interest and Sinking Fund" to pay the interest when due, the State Board of Land Commissioners and the State Board of Examiners shall by an order entered on their minutes or record books, cause warrants to be issued on the said "Deaf and Dumb Asylum Interest and Sinking Fund" for the amount of interest due, and the warrants so issued shall be registered in the office of the Treasurer of the State, and shall bear interest at the rate of six per cent per annum ,and said warrants shall be paid by the State Treasurer whenever there is sufficient money accumulated in said fund to pay the same; and by reason of the delivery of said warrants to the holders of said bonds and the surrender of the interest coupons, there shall be no default in the payment of interest.

Section 11. Nothing in this Act shall be so construed as to in any wise hold the State of Montana liable for the payment of the bonds herein authorized or the interest thereon, except as to the lien heretofore created against the lands and funds granted for the purpose of erecting a Deaf and Dumb Asylum, and which lien shall not be abridged, annulled or set aside until the bonds authorized by this act shall have been fully paid, together with the interest thereon, and the Governor is hereby specially authorized and empowered to use all lawful means to enforce the provisions of this act.

Section 12. All acts and parts of acts in conflict with this act are hereby repealed.

Section 13. There is hereby appropriated from the proceeds of the sale of the bonds authorized by this Act, the sum of sixty-five thousand dollars ($65,000.00) for the fiscal year ending December first, 1897.

Section 14. This act shall be in full force and effect from and after its passage and approval by the Governor.

(Act approved March 4, 1897.)

SUBSTITUTE FOR HOUSE BILL NO. 69.

An Act to Establish County Free High Schools and to Provide for Their Maintenance.

Section 1. Any county in the State may establish a county free high school on the conditions and in the manner hereinafter prescribed, for the purpose of affording better educational facilities for pupils more advanced than those attending district schools.

Section 2. Whenever two hundred school electors in any county shall petition the Board of County Commissioners requesting that a county high school be established in their county at a place in the said petition named, or whenever the said County Commissioners shall at their discretion think proper, they shall give twenty days' notice that they will submit the question to the school electors of said county whether such high school shall be established, and at the place specified, at which election the school electors of the county shall vote by ballot for or against establishing such high school. The notices shall distinctly specify the city, town or district wherein it is proposed to establish said high school.

Section 3. The election shall be conducted in all respects the same as the election for school trustees, except that the County Commissioners shall call the election, and that there shall be no registration of voters required. After said election, the ballots on said question shall be canvassed in the same manner as in the election for county officers, and if a majority of all the votes cast shall be in favor of establishing such high school, the County Commissioners shall immediately proceed to appoint six persons, who shall be residents and taxpayers of the county, three of whom shall be residents of the township where the school is located, who shall with the county superintendent of schools constitute a Board of Trustees for said school. Each of said trustees appointed as aforesaid shall hold office until his successor is appointed and qualified, and shall be required within ten days after appointment to qualify by taking the usual oath of office, and by giving such bond as may be required by said County Commissioners for the faithful discharge of his duties.

Section 4. Said trustees shall be divided into three classes of two each, the term of office of each class to be one, two and three years respectively, the respective terms to be decided by lot. The term of office of those in the first class shall expire one year from the third Saturday in April following their appointment; the term of those in the second class shall expire two years from the third Saturday in April following their appointment, and the term of office of those in the third class shall expire three years from the third Saturday in April following their appointment.

The County Commissioners shall appoint trustees in place of those whose term expires or in case of vacancy. The term of office of trustees shall be for three years.

In case of vacancy the appointment shall be for the remainder of the unexpired term. Provided, that in all appointments of trustees under this Act there shall be one trustee in each class who is a resident of the township in which said high school is located.

Said board of high school trustees shall be governed, as to the time and place of meeting, by the provisions of the general school law of the State.

Section 5: A majority of said board shall constitute a quorum for the transaction of all business, but four votes shall be required to decide any question.

Section 6. At their first meeting in each year the trustees shall choose from their number a president, secretary and treasurer, who shall hold office for one year, or until their successors are appointed and qualified. Said treasurer shall give such additional bond as the County Commissioners shall deem sufficient. And said trustees shall have authority to make all necessary rules for their government not inconsistent with the law.

Section 7. At said first meeting, or at some succeeding meeting called for such purpose, said trustees shall make an estimate of the amount of funds needed for building purposes, for payment of teachers' wages, and for payment of contingent expenses, and they shall present to the Board of County Commissioners a certified estimate of the rate of tax required to raise the amount desired for such purpose. But in no case shall the tax for such purpose exceed in one year the amount of ten mills on the dollar on the taxable property of the county, and when the tax is levied for the payment of teachers' wages and for contingent expenses only, it shall not exceed three mills on the dollar. Provided, that said trustees may, if in their judgment they think best, bond the county for the purpose of raising the money necessary to build and equip the high school herein provided for and to purchase a suitable site therefor. But no bonds shall ever be issued to pay for teachers' salaries or for the general expenses in maintaining said school.

Section 8. Whenever any board of trustees of any county free high school shall decide to bond the county as provided in the foregoing Section said trustees shall issue said bonds in the manner provided for the issuance of school district bonds. Provided, that no county shall be bonded for the above purpose in an amount to exceed one hundred thousand dollars.

Section 9. Said bonds shall be paid, principal and interest, in the manner provided for the payment for school district bonds.

Section 10. In case bonds are issued then the trustees in making estimates for the maintenance of the high school shall not include estimates for building or whatever said bonds are issued for.

Section 11. Said tax shall be levied and collected in the same manner as other county taxes, and when collected the county treasurer shall pay the same to the treasurer of the county high school.

Section 12. The said treasurer of the high school shall receive from the county treasurer, and from all other parties, all monies that belong to the fund of said high school, and shall pay out the same only by direction of the Board of Trustees, upon orders duly signed by the president and countersigned by the secretary, stating the purpose for which they were drawn. Both the secretary and treasurer shall keep an accurate account of all monies received and expended for said school, and at the close of each year, or oftener if required by the Board of Trustees, they shall make a full statement of the financial affairs of the school.

Section 13. The said board of trustees shall proceed, as soon as practicable after the appointment as aforesaid, to select at the place determined by the vote of the county, the best site that can be obtained and the title thereof shall be vested in the said county; they shall then proceed to make purchases of material and to let such contracts for their necessary school buildings as they may deem proper, but shall not make any purchase or contract in any year to exceed the amount on hand, and to be raised by the levy of tax or issue of bonds for that year. The Board of Trustees at their discretion may lease suitable buildings for the use of the high school while new buildings are in process of erection, or may, if in their judgment they deem it best, contract with the trustees of the district at the county seat for the use of any suitable building for a high school for such time as they deem for the best interests of the county.

Section 14. When such Board of Trustees shall have provided for the county free high school contemplated in this Act, they shall employ some suitable person, who shall take charge of the same, and teach in the same, and shall be known as the principal of such school; and the trustees shall furnish such assistant teachers as they deem necessary, and shall provide for their salaries.

Section 15. The principal of any such high school, with the approval of the Board of Trustees, shall make such rules and regulations as he may deem proper in regard to the studies, conduct and government of the pupils under his charge; and if any such pupils will not conform to nor obey the rules of the school, they may be suspended or expelled therefrom by the Board of Trustees.

Section 16. There shall be provided such courses of study as will properly fit the student attending said high school for admission to the freshman class of any of the State educational institutions, and shall contain the work provided for accredited high schools by the State Board of Education.

Section 17. Tuition shall be free to all pupils residing in the county where the school is located. The Board of Trustees shall make such general rules and regulations as they deem proper in regard to age and grade of attainments essential to entitle pupils to admission to such school; provided, that no person shall be admitted to such high school who shall not have passed a satisfactory examination or who does not hold an eighth-grade common school certificate. If there should be more applicants than can be accommodated at any one time, each district shall be entitled to send its equal proportion of pupils, according to the number of pupils it may have, as shown by the last report to the county superintendent of public instruction; and the boards of the respective school districts shall designate such pupils as may attend, subject to the proviso above.

Section 18. If at any time the school can accommodate more pupils than apply for admission from the county in which the school is situated, the vacancies may be filled by applications from other counties upon the payment of such tuition as the Board of Trustees may prescribe; but at no time shall such pupils continue in such school to the exclusion of pupils residing in the county in which such school is situated.

Section 19. The trustees shall serve without compensation and shall make such reports to the County Superintendent as he may require or as may be required by the Superintendent of Public Instruction.

Section 20. Upon the presentation of a certificate of graduation from any such county high school, within one year from the date of the same, to any State institution of learning, the person presenting the same may be admitted without further examination to said institution of learning.

Section 21. The County Commissioners of any county of Montana be and they are hereby authorized to negotiate with the school district at the county seat of such county for the establishment of a county high school.

Section 22. For the purpose of carrying this Act into effect the Board of County Comissioners in such counties may employ such number of teachers in addition to those regularly employed by the district at the county seat, as shall in their judgment be necessary for the purpose of conducting such schools, and pay such teachers from the general fund of the county. Provided the management of such high school shall be under the trustees of said district.

Section 23. Such county high school shall be free to all persons of school age in their respective counties.

Section 24. All Acts and parts of Acts in conflict with the provisions of this act are hereby repealed.

(Act approved March 3rd, 1899.)

HOUSE BILL NO. 16.

An Act to Empower the Board of School Trustees of Any District to Establish and Maintain Free Kindergartens for the Instruction of Children Between Three and Six Years of Age.

Section 1. The school board of any school district in the State shall have power to establish and maintain free kindergartens in connection with the public schools of said district, for the instruction of children between three and six years of age, residing in said district and shall establish such courses of training, study and discipline, and such rules and regulations governing such preparatory or kindergarten schools as said board may deem best; Provided, That nothing in this act shall be construed to change the law relating to the taking of the census of the school population or the apportionment of state and county school funds among the several counties and districts in this State; Provided, further, That the cost of establishing and maintaining such kindergartens shall be paid from the school funds of said districts, and the said kindergartens shall be a part of the public school system and governed as far as practicable in the same manner and by the same officers as is now, or hereafter may be, provided by law for the government of the other public schools of the State; Provided, further, That the teachers of kindergarten schools shall pass such examination on kindergarten work as the kindergarten department of the State Normal School may direct, provided that a certificate from a kindergarten teachers' institute of recognized standing shall be recognized by the State Normal School.

*Section 2. All Acts and parts of Acts inconsistent with the provisions of this Act are hereby repealed.

(Act approved February 16th, 1899.)

CHAPTER XIII.

Forms for Use of School Officers.

No. 1.

CERTIFICATE OF ELECTION OF TRUSTEE.

To....................of..................Greeting:

This is to certify that at a...................School Meeting of School District No....of...............County, held at the School House of said District, ...1...., you were duly elected to fill the office of trustee for the term of...............

Section 1782 of the Political Code reads as follows:

Trustees elected shall take office immediately after qualifying and shall hold office for the term of three years and until their successors are elected and qualified, or appointed by the County Superintendent of Schools and qualified. Every trustee elected shall file his or her oath of office with the County Superintendent of Schools. Any trustee who shall fail to qualify within fifteen days after being elected shall forfeit all right to office, and the County Superintendent of Schools shall appoint to fill the vacancy.

....
Clerk of School District Meeting.

OATH OF OFFICE.

I do solemnly swear (or affirm) that I will support, protect and defend the Constitution of the United States, and the Constitution of the State of Montana, and that I will discharge the duties of my office with fidelity; and that I have not paid or contributed, or promised to pay, or contribute, either directly or indirectly, any money or other valuable thing to procure my nomination or election (or appointment) except for necessary and proper expenses expressly authorized by law; that I have not knowingly violated any election law of this State, or procured it to be done by others in my behalf; that I will not knowingly receive directly or indirectly any money or other valuable thing for the performance or non-performance of any act or duty pertaining to my office other than the compensation allowed by law. So help me God.

....
Subscribed and sworn to before me, this......day of......1....
....

Note.—This oath must be taken before some one authorized to administer oaths.

No. 2.

CERTIFICATE OF APPOINTMENT OF TRUSTEE.

To....................of..................Greeting:

This is to certify that I have this...........day of..........1...
appointed...................of.................County, to fill the office of Trustee, until the next annual election of said district.

Section 1782 of the Political Code reads as follows:

Trustees elected shall take office immediately after qualifying and shall hold office for the term of three years and until their successors are elected and qualified, or appointed by the County Superintendent of Schools and qualified. Every trustee elected shall file his or her oath of office with the County Superintendent of Schools. Any trustee who shall fail to qualify within fifteen days after being elected shall forfeit all rights to office, and the County Superintendent of Schools shall appoint to fill the vacancy.

....
County Superintendent.

Remarks.—This Certificate, with oath of office endorsed thereon, signed and sworn to before some person competent to administer oaths, must be sent to the County Superintendent.

OATH OF OFFICE.

I do solemnly swear (or affirm) that I will support, protect and defend the Constitution of the United States, and the Constitution of the State of Montana, and that I will discharge the duties of my office with fidelity; and that I have not paid or contributed, or promised to pay, or contribute, either directly or indirectly, any money or other valuable thing to procure my nomination or election (or appointment) except for necessary and proper expenses expressly authorized by law; that I have not knowingly violated any election law of this State, or procured it to be done by others in my behalf; that I will not knowingly receive directly or indirectly any money or other valuable thing for the performance or non-performance of any act or duty pertaining to my office other than the compensation allowed by law. So help me God.

....
Subscribed and sworn to before me, this......day of......1....
....

Remarks.—This oath may be taken before any school officer or other person competent to administer oaths.

No. 3.

CERTIFICATE OF APPOINTMENT OF CLERK.

To......................of.................Greeting:

This is to certify that at a*.....................School meeting of School District No....of........................County, held ....1...., you were duly appointed to fill the office of District Clerk to serve during the pleasure of the Board.

If you accept, please take the oath of office hereto attached, and return this notice to the Trustees without delay.

..............................)
..............................} Trustees for District No.......
..............................)

*State whether "Regular" or "Special" Meeting.

Remarks.—This certificate, with oath of office endorsed thereon, signed and sworn to before some person competent to administer oaths, must be sent to County Superintendent after receipt by the Trustees.

OATH OF OFFICE.

I do solemnly swear (or affirm) that I will support, protect and defend the Constitution of the United States, and the Constitution of the State of Montana, and that I will discharge the duties of my office with fidelity; and that I have not paid or contributed, or promised to pay, or contribute, either directly or indirectly, any money or other valuable thing to procure my nomination or election (or appointment) except for necessary and proper expenses expressly authorized by law; that I have not knowingly violated any election law of this State, or procured it to be done by others in my behalf; that I will not knowingly receive directly or indirectly any money or other valuable thing for the performance or non-performance of any act or duty pertaining to my office other than the compensation allowed by law. So help me God.

....
Subscribed and sworn to before me, this......day of......1....
....
....

Remarks.—This oath may be taken before any school officer or other person competent to administer oaths.

No. 4.

AGREEMENT BETWEEN SCHOOL TRUSTEES AND TEACHER.

This agreement, made and entered into this................day of...................., A. D. 1...., between.................... party of the first part, and the School Trustees of School District No...., of......................County, Montana, parties of the second part,

Witnesseth, that the said......................., who holds a legal certificate as teacher for said county, hereby agrees, for the consideration hereafter stated, to teach the school in said district for the period of..............months, commencing on the..........day of..................., 1...., and said....................further agrees to enforce the rules and regulations prescribed by the Superintendent of Public Instruction and the County Superintendent; to strictly follow the advice of the County Superintendent given within his or her authority; to use only such text-books as are prescribed by law; and to keep a school register and make the returns prescribed by law.

And the parties of the second part hereby agree to pay the said ...., ...Dollars for each and every month of twenty school days, in the manner following, to-wit: By drawing their order upon the County Treasurer of said County, to be paid out of any school moneys in the County Treasury standing to the credit of said District.

It is mutually understood and agreed that whenever the school shall be closed by order of the Trustees on account of the prevalence of contagious or epidemic disease, or from any cause, the salary of said first party as teacher shall.. ....

In witness whereof the said parties have hereunto set their hands and seals in duplicate at the date hereinbefore mentioned.

....
Teacher.
....
....
....
Trustees of School District No....
..................County.

Note.—Fill out the blank at close of contract in accordance with your agreement on this point. If the teacher is to receive her salary when school is closed, then add, "be paid the same as when school is in session," or, if no salary is to be paid, then add, "cease for such time as the school is closed." or such words as shall clearly express your agreement. Each party should have a copy of the contract.

No. 5.
TEACHER'S REPORT.

Teacher's report of the public schools in District No....... in the County of.................., Montana, from the.............. day of................., 1...., to the................. day of ...., 1....

Whole number scholars enrolled during term	....
Whole number of days taught	....
Average number actually belonging..	....
Average daily attendance	....
Percentage of attendance	....
Total number of days attendance...	....
Total number of times tardy...	....
Total number of days absent	....
Total number between 8 and 14 attending school	....
Total number from other districts attending school	....
Number cases corporal punishment..	....
Grade of school	....
Number of classes in school	....
Date of teacher taking charge of school.................................	....
Date of closing term of school	....
Monthly salary of teacher	....
Amount of salary from county school fund................................	....
Grade and date of teacher's certificate..................................	....
Number of school visits by school trustee...............................	....
Number of school visits by County Superintendent	....
Number of school visits by other parties................................	....
Have you kept School Register as Required?	....
Have you used prescribed series of text books?	....
Have you followed prescribed course of study?	....
Have you complied with provisions of School Law relating to duties of teachers?..	....
Is your school provided with maps, globes, reading charts?..............	....
Is your school provided with Physiology charts?	....
What are the needs of your school?......................................	....
Are you a graduate of a normal school?..................................	....
Have you ever attended a normal school?.................................	....
If so, for what length of time?...	....
Has your district a school library?.....................................	....
How many volumes were bought for it last year?	....

N. B.—Section 1841 of the Political Code requires this report to be made, annually, to the County Superintendent and District Clerk on or before the 10th day of September next after the close of each school year—August 31.

Any teacher who shall close any term of school before the close of the school year shall make a report to the County Superintendent immediately after the close of such term, and any teacher who may be teaching any school at the close of the school year, shall, in his or her annual report, include all statistics from the school register for the entire school year, notwithstanding any previous report for a part of the year.

Trustees are not allowed, under the law, to draw any warrant for the teacher's salary for the last month of school until all the reports herein required shall have been made and received.

In districts having a city superintendent these reports are made to him and the city superintendent will make up the report of the districts for the county superintendent. Where there is no city superintendent, but a principal of the schools, his report will be acccepted in lieu of the teachers' reports.

To find the "Average Daily Attendance" for the term or the year, divide the whole number of days' attendance by the number of days taught. To find the "Per Cent. of Attendance" for the term or year, divide the whole number of days' of attendance by the sum of the whole number of days' attendance plus the whole number of days of absence.

No. 6.

COUNTY CLERK AND RECORDER'S REPORT.

Required under Section 1890, Political Code, to be returned to the County Superintendent of Schools during the month of September, of each year.

Assessed valuation of.........................County for year 1.......
Rate of taxation for school purposes............ ....
Amount to be apportioned ....

I, ... Clerk and Recorder of.............. County, State of Montana, hereby certify that the above report is correct.

....
Clerk and Recorder.

Dated........................, 1....

No. 7.

REPORT OF CLERK OF DISTRICT COURT OF..............
County.

Required under Section 1891, Political Code, to be returned to County Superintendent of Schools at close of Every Term of Court.

	Date of Fine.	Amount of Fine.

To................., County Superintendent of Schools:

I hereby certify that the above report of fines imposed by Judge .... of .... District Court, for term ending on........................,....., 1...., is true and correct.

....
Clerk of...............District Court.
Dated......................., 1....

No. 8.

REPORT OF.....................JUSTICE OF THE PEACE
For..................Precinct..................County.

Required under Section 1892, Political Code, to be Returned to the County Superintendent of Schools During the Month of September of each Year.

	Fines Imposed.	Fines Collected	When Paid to Co Treasurer.

To...................County Superintendent of Schools:

I hereby certify that the above report of fines imposed, collected, and date when paid to County Treasurer, is true and correct.

....
Justice of the Peace.

Dated....................,., 1....

No. 9.

COUNTY TREASURER'S REPORT.

Subdivision 4 of Section 1880 of the Political Code, referring to the duties of County Treasurer, provides:

"Fourth. To make annually during the month of October in each year, a financial report for the last school year and fiscal year ending with June 30, to the Superintendent of Common Schools, in such form as may be required by him."

Note.—"October" should read September; "June 30" should read August 31.

NET RECEIPTS FOR SCHOOL PURPOSES FOR YEAR ENDING AUG. 31, 1....

	Dollars.	Cts
Amount received from—		
County Tax		
Special District Tax		
Clerk of District Court		
District Court		
Justices of Peace		
All Other Sources		
Total amount received from all sources.............		

	Amount to Credit of District at Beginning of Year.		Amount Apportioned During Year.		Amount of Orders Paid During Year.		Amount to Credit of District at End of Year.	
	Dollars	Cts	Dollars	Cts	Dollars	Cts	Dollars	Cts
School District No.—								
1...								
2...								
3...								
4...								
5...								
6...								
7...								
8...								
9...								
10...								
11...								
12...								
13...								
14...								
15...								
16...								
17...								
18...								
19...								
20...								
21...								
22...								
23...								
24...								
25...								
26...								
27...								
28...								
29...								
30...								
31...								
32...								
33...								

34...					
35...					
36...					
37...					
38...					
39...					
40...					
41...					
42...					
43...					
44...					
45...					
46...					
47...					
48...					
49...					
50...					

I, ... Treasurer of the County of.............., Montana, hereby certify that the foregoing is a correct financial exhibit of all moneys received, paid out, and now held by said County for school purposes for the year ending August 31, 1..... .

....

County Treasurer.

Dated ....

No. 10.

NOTICE OF ELECTION.

The Annual Meeting

of School District No...., ... County, Montana, for the election of......................Trustee..will be held on Saturday, April................, 1...., at the District School House. The polls will be open between the hours of........... and......... o'clock ....m.

........................)
........................) Trustees.
........................)

Dated ...., 1....

No. 11.

NOTICE OF ELECTION.

A Special Meeting

of School District No...., ...County, Montana, for the purpose of.. will be held on the...............the...............day of.......... 1...., at the District School House. The polls will be open between the hours of ....and...........o'clock, ...m.

..........................)
..........................) Trustees.
..........................)

Dated ...., 1....

No. 12.
CENSUS.

Follow these instructions very carefully, and thus avoid mistakes.

Subdivision 3, Section 1830, of the Political Code, reads:

"The school clerk shall take, annually, between the first and twentieth days of August of each year an exact census of all the children and youth between the ages of six and twenty-one years residing in the district, and shall specify the number and sex of such children, and the names of their parents or guardians. He shall take specifically and separately, a census of all children under six years of age, and shall specify the number and sex of such children. All children under twenty-one years of age who may be absent from home for any cause shall be included by the district clerk in this census list of the city, town or district in which their parents reside. He shall make a full report thereof on the blanks furnished for this purpose under oath to the County Superintendent thereafter, and deliver a copy to the school trustees."

If the Clerk fails or neglects to take the census as above he is liable to the district.

List no children unless their parents or guardians reside in your district at the time the census is taken. Children attending school in your district whose parents reside in another district or whose parents are living temporarily in your district, for the purpose of sending their children to school, but whose legal residence is elsewhere, cannot be listed. Such children will be listed in the district where their parents have their legal residence.

In all cases the legal residence of the parents determines the district in which the children must be enumerated.

The census can only be taken between the first and twentieth days of August.

SCHOOL CENSUS REPORT.

Report of .... District Clerk of
School District No ...., ... County, Montana.

NAMES OF CHILDREN.	AGE	SEX		AGE	SEX		Occupation if Not Attending School	NAME OF PARENT OR GUARDIAN.
	Between 6 and 21	Male	Female	Under Six	Male	Female		
....	...	...	...	...	...	...	....	....
....	...	...	...	...	...	...	....	....
....	...	...	...	...	...	...	....	....
....	...	...	...	...	...	...	....	....
....	...	...	...	...	...	...	....	....
....	...	...	...	...	...	...	....	....
....	...	...	...	...	...	...	....	....
....	...	...	...	...	...	...	....	....
....	...	...	...	...	...	...	....	....
....	...	...	...	...	...	...	....	....
....	...	...	...	...	...	...	....	....
....	...	...	...	...	...	...	....	....
....	...	...	...	...	...	...	....	....
....	...	...	...	...	...	...	....	....
Totals	...	...	...	...	...	...	....	....

SUMMARY.

	Male.	Female	Total.
Total Number of Children in the District, between 6 and 14..	....	....	....
Total Number of Children in the District, between 14 and 18..	....	....	....
Total Number of Children in the District, between 18 and 21..	....	....	....
Total Number of Children in the District, between 6 and 21..	....	....	....
Total Number of Children in the District, under 6 yrs. of age	....	....	....
Total	....	....	....

STATE OF MONTANA,)
.... County,) ss.

I, ..., being first duly sworn, depose and say that I am clerk of School District No ......, in the County of ...., State of Montana; that the foregoing is a true and correct census of the children of said District, as required by law, taken by me between the 1st and 20th days of August, A. D ......

....
Clerk's Signature.

Subscribed and sworn to before me this .... day of ...., A. D. 1 ......

....
....

CENSUS OF DEAF, BLIND AND FEEBLE-MINDED.

Section 2345 of the Political Code reads:

The school district clerk of each county in this State shall annually report to the county superintendent of schools the names, ages and postoffice addresses, and the names of parents or guardians, of every deaf or blind or feeble-minded person between the ages of five (5) and twenty-one (21) years residing in said school district, including all who are too deaf or blind to obtain an education in the public school.

The county superintendent of public schools shall, on or before the first day of August of each year, send a complete list of the names, ages and addresses of all such persons in said county to the superintendent of the school for the defective.

Report of School District No...., ...County, Montana.

Names of Children.	Age Between 5-21.	Deaf.	Blind.	Feeble Minded.	Parent or Guardian.	Post Office.
....	......	......	......	......	....	....
....	......	......	......	......	....	....
....	......	......	......	......	....	....
....	......	......	......	......	....	....
....	......	......	......	......	....	....
....	......	......	......	......	....	....
....	......	......	......	......	....	....
....	......	......	......	......	....	....
....	......	......	......	......	....	....
....	......	......	......	......	....	....
....	......	......	......	......	....	....
Total	......	......	......	......	....	....

STATE OF MONTANA,)
) ss.
.... County.)

I, ..., being first duly sworn, depose and say that I am Clerk of School District No........, in the County of ...., State of Montana; that the foregoing is a true and correct census of the deaf, blind and feeble-minded children residing in said district, taken by me between the 1st and 20th days of August, ...

                              ....
                                       Clerk's Signature.

Subscribed and sworn to before me this......day of......, 1....
                 ....

INDEX.

	Sec.	Page
BOARD OF TEXT-BOOK COMMISSIONERS—		
of whom to consist	1	87
when and where to meet	2	87
to appoint a secretary	2	87
SUPERINTENDENT OF PUBLIC INSTRUCTION—		
to advertise date of meeting	3	87
to receive proposals for supply of books	3	87
books to be adopted	3	87
duty of Commissioners	4	88
power of Commissioners	5	88
contract with publishers	6	89
bond to be approved by Governor	6	89
failure of publishers to perform obligations	7	89
prices of book to be furnished County Superintendents	8	90
failure to use books prescribed	9	90
trustees or clerks to report annually on text-books	10	90
voters may petition board of trustees	11	90
vote on question of free text-books	11	90
board of trustees must notify voters of election	11	90
special tax levy to pay for text-books	12	90
mileage and per diem	13	91
appropriation to pay mileage and per diem	13	91
BONDS—DEAF AND DUMB ASYLUM—		
to pay building warrants	1	98
amount to be issued, denominations; time to run	3	99
rate of interest; where payable; form; coupons	1	98
by whom disposed of	2	99
fund created for payment of interest	3	99
fund created for payment of principal	4	99
to be paid in order of issuance	8	101
cost of issuance to be paid out of proceeds	9	101
warrants to issue in payment of interest	10	101
State not liable	11	101
BONDS—SCHOOL OF MINES—		
who to issue; amount; denomination; term; rate of interest; place of payment; form; coupons	1	94
how disposed of	2	95
interest and sinking fund	3	95
permanent fund, how created and in what invested	4	95
if interest paid from general fund, State to be reimbursed	5	96
State Treasurer custodian of funds	6	96
to pay outstanding warrants	7	96
paid in order of their issuance	8	96
cost of issuance to be paid out of proceeds	9	96
if not sufficient funds to pay interest, warrants to be drawn	10	97
State not liable	11	97

INDEX:

	Sec.	Page
BONDS—UNIVERSITY OF MONTANA—		
time to run	1	91
rate of interest	1	91
denominations	1	91
when to be sold	2	94
fund created for payment	3	94
State Treasurer to pay cost of issue, interest, etc	4	94
State Treasurer must give notice	5	93
moneys derived from sale of, how used	6	93
Building Commission	7	93
State not liable	8	93
CENSUS OF SCHOOL CHILDREN—		
contents of	1830	52
compensation for taking	1830	53
district clerk to make	1830	53
district clerk, liability for not taking	1830	53
report of county superintendent	1830	53
CITY SUPERINTENDENT OF SCHOOLS—		
appointed when	1930	66
duties of	1932	66
qualification	1931	66
work in conflict	1933	66
CLERK OF DISTRICT COURT—		
superintendent to report to, fines imposed by court	1891	58
penalty	1893	59
COMPULSORY ATTENDANCE—		
clerk must furnish list	1922	65
excuses for non-compliance	1920	64
parents required to send children to school	1920	64
penalty	1921	65
procedure	1925	66
prosecution	1923	65
truant officer	1924	65
COUNTY CLERK—		
to report to County Superintendent tax levied	1890	58
penalty	1893	59
COUNTY SUPERINTENDENT OF SCHOOLS—		
blanks, distribution by	1733	28
bond of	1730	28
boundaries of school district	1741	30
certificates, temporary, may issue	1739	29
controversies, decides	1735	29
district clerk, makes report of census to	1830	52
election	1730	28
examinations, public, must hold for certificates	1910	60
fines, reported to	1891	58
institutes, teachers' must hold	1900	59
institutes, presides at	1738	29
oath of	1730	28
oaths, may administer	1736	29
office, stationery for	1742	30
powers, general of	1731	28
qualification of	1744	30

	Sec.	Page
report, annual of	1740	30
records, of official acts kept by	1734	29
schols, supervision of	1731	28
schools, must visit twice a year	1732	28
school money, apportions	1737	29
teach, must not	1743	30
term of	1730	28
text-books, forfeiting of school fund for not using certain	1758	34
trustee, appoints, when	1980	75

COUNTY TREASURER—

	Sec.	Page
duties of as to school bonds	1968	75
duties as to school funds	1880	58

DISTRICT CLERK—

	Sec.	Page
Census, to make	1830	52
Census, contents of	1830	52
Census, report of to county superintendent	1830	52
Census, compensation for making	1830	52
Census, liability for not making	1830	52
duties of	1830	52
fines, imposed by court to report to county superintendent	1891	58
penalty for failure to report	1893	59
pupils, must furnish list of, to trustees	1922	65
report to county superintendent list of deaf and dumb and blind children in district	2345	83

DEAF AND DUMB ASYLUM—

	Sec.	Page
admittance to, regulation of	2342	82
admittance of feeble-minded children	2346	84
admittance of non-residents	2343	83
board of officers of, meeting	2333	80
board of trustees, control	2332	80
board of, duties of	2334	80
board of, oath of	2335	81
board of, compensation and secretary	2337	81
by-laws	2351	85
contracts, officers not interested in	2341	82
employes, privileges of	2340	82
fund of	2354	86
funds, how expended	2347	84
lands set apart for	2353	86
location of	2330	79
objects	2331	79
pauper inmates of	2344	83
records of	2336	81
reports of	2352	85
school district clerks, duties as to	2345	83
school, term of	2349	84
State Board of Education, powers of, as to	2348	84
superintendent of	2338	81
superintendent, powers and duties of	2339	82
trustee, removal of	2350	85

EXAMINATIONS AND CERTIFICATES—

	Sec.	Page
grades, number and term of certificates	1911	61
proficiency in certain grades required	1911	61

	Sec.	Page
qualification of principal of high school	1911	61
temporary certificates may be granted	1911	62
recourse of candidate who thinks injustice has been done	1911	62
age at which certificate may be issued	1912	63
where certificates are valid	1912	63
per cent. of proficiency required	1912	63
certificates, fees paid for	1913	63
certificates, County Superintendent may revoke, when	1914	63
County superintendent to hold public, for	1910	60
questions for	1915	64

JUSTICE OF THE PEACE—

	Sec.	Page
to report fines collected by	1892	59
penalty	1893	59
Free High School		102
Free Kindergarten		106

PUPILS—

	Sec.	Page
abuse of, misdemeanor	1846	55
compulsory attendance of		64-66
expulsion of	1870	57
insult to teacher	2022	78
moral training	1845	55
regulations, must comply with	1870	57
suspension of	1844	55

SCHOOLS—

	Sec.	Page
age of admission to	1860	56
common, defined	1860	56
common, hours of	1862	57
common, sectarian publications forbidden in	1863	57
common schol month, length of	1843	55
common school year	1864	57
county attorney, duty of	2027	79
course of study in	1861	56
disturbing	2023	78
English language taught in	1861	56
fines, how collected and when paid	2021	78
meaning of words	2020	78
penalties	2028	79
printing and binding	2024	78
pupils must obey regulation	1870	58
pupils, expulsion of	1870	57
School day, length of	1862	57
school officers, oath of	2026	78
teacher or officer, not to act as agent	2025	78
teacher, penalty for acting as agent	2025	78
teacher, insult to	2023	78

SCHOOL BONDS—

	Sec.	Page
ballots, form of	1962	72
County Treasurer, duty of	1870	57
district liable for	1964	73
issued how, election, limitation	1960	71
penalty	1970	75
preparing and printing	1969	75
redemption, order of	1967	74
redemption, notice of	1967	74
sale of, notice	1963	72

INDEX.

	Sec.	Page
tax levy, for interest on	1965	73
tax levy, for interest and redemption of	1966	73
trustees failing to pay money from sale of	1970	75
SCHOOL BUILDINGS—		
provided with American flags	1807-9	49
SCHOOL DISTRICTS—		
apportionment of money to, three months' school necessary	1757	34
bodies, corporate, are	1759	34
boundaries	1752	32
created, when	1760	34
defined	1750	31
district in two counties	1755	33
division of district funds and property	1754	33
new, apportionment of money to	1753	32
organization of new	1751	31
SCHOOL FUNDS—		
Apportionment of	1942	69
building and furnishing fund	1946	70
lots, proceeds of town	1945	70
road funds, transfer of	1944	69
school tax, how collected	1941	69
state	1940(a)	67
taxation, election	1940(b)	67
transfer, election	1948	70
use of	1943	69
warrants	1947	70
SCHOOL LAWS—		
Superintendent of Public Instruction to publish	1709	25
SCHOOL LIBRARIES—		
fund for	2000	77
fund for, how formed	2001-2	77
fund, control of	2003	77
selecction of books for	2005	77
trustees of, duties	2004	77
SCHOOL OF MINES—		
established	1572	16
trustees, term, quorum	1573	16
appointment of trustees	1574	16
oath	1575	17
powers of trustees	1576	17
objects	1577	17
site, appliances	1578	17
students, qualification of	1579	17
officers of board	1580	17
vacancies, how filled	1581	17
report	1582	18
school lands, location of	1583	18
revenue of school	1584	18
donations, investment of	1585	19
Treasurer, bond of	1586	19
professors, fees of	1587	19
debt prohibited	1588	19
faculty of school	1589	19
donations, trustees may accept	1590	19

	Sec.	Page
SUPERINTENDENT OF PUBLIC INSTRUCTION—		
appeals, files in office all papers concerning	1708	25
blanks, etc., to prepare	1703	25
bond	1700	24
clerk, may appoint	1715	27
course of study	1705	25
county superintendents, duties as to	1707	25
duties of	1701	25
election	1700	24
examinations	1704	25
expenses of	1707	25
oath	1700	24
powers, general	1702	25
qualification	1700	24
record of official acts	1708	25
report of	1712	26
report of, number to be published	1513	10
report, distribution of	1713	26
salary of	1716	27
school fund, must apportion	1714	27
school laws, printing of	1709	25
seal, official of	1710	26
teachers' institute, rules as to	1706	25
teachers' institute must attend	1711	26
STATE AGRICULTURAL COLLEGE—		
control and management of	1624	21
establishment of	1622	20
experimental station of	1628	21
experimental station, management of	1629	22
executive board, officers of	1626	21
secrtary and treasurer of board	1627	21
STATE BOARD OF EDUCATION—		
appointment and term	1511	9
diploma, state	1517	11
diploma, life	1518	11
diploma, revocation of	1520	12
expenses	1521	12
meetings of	1515	10
membership of	1510	9
oath of	1512	10
officers of	1513	10
powers and duties	1516	10
quorum	1514	10
STATE NORMAL SCHOOL—		
acceptance of public lands	1655	22
control, management and suspension	1654	22
establishment	1652	22
executive board	1656	22
objects of	1653	22
graduates may teach without examination		23
graduates entitled to diploma		23
STATE UNIVERSITY—		
appropriation for	1553	14
charges for tuition	1551	14
education, state board of, duty and power of	1545	12

	Sec.	Page
endowed professorships established	1543	12
government, officers	1544	12
location of	1543	12
military instruction	1550	14
objects of	1548	13
officers of university, report of	1547	13
selection of site	1544	12
students, qualification of	1550	14
study, course of	1549	14

TEACHERS—

	Sec.	Page
age of	1847	56
agents, must not act as, penalty	2025	78
contract with	1843	55
dismissal of appeal	1848	56
duties, regular of	1842	54
employed, of	1842	54
examinations and certificates of	1910-1915	60-64
moral training, duties of as to	1845	55
pupil, may suspend, when	1844	55
pupils, abuse	1846	55
pupils, insult to teacher	2022	78
qualifications of	1840	54
report of	1841	54
school month	1843	55
unprofessional conduct of	1849	56

TEACHERS' INSTITUTE—

	Sec.	Page
certain counties in	1901	59
county superintendent must hold	1900	59
expenses of	1905	60
fund for	1904	60
sessions of	1902	59
teachers must attend	1903	59

TREE PLANTING—

	Sec.	Page
Arbor Day, second Tuesday in May	1990	76
Arbor Day, tree planting on, by school children	1991	76
exercises, superintendent opens services	1992	76

TRUSTEES—

	Sec.	Page
board, powers concerning bonds	1810	50
board of, powers, quorum, term	1790-91	45
board of, organization	1793	45
board of, general meetings of	1794	45
board of, chairman, rules	1796	46
board of, powers of and duties	1797	46
board of, duties of as to privies	1798-99	47-48
board, powers of as to property	1801	48
board of, liability of	1803	48
board, may establish high school	1804	48
board, failure to deliver books to successors	1805	49
board, repayment of loan by	1806	49
board, district, to attend all meetings of	1830	52
board, disposal of proceeds of bonds	1811	51
board, redemption of	1814	51
bonds, payment of interest	1815	52
bonds, preparation of	1816	52
contract, must not be interested in	1802	48
contract of, with teacher, how construed	1843	55
districts of, new	1792	45

INDEX.

	Sec.	Page
district, responsible on bonds	1812	51
election of	1770	35
annual; time and place of; classification of districts; term of office..	1770	35
districts of first class under supervision of county commissioners	1771	35
second and third class under supervision of trustees	1772	36
clerk to post notices; trustees to appoint judges	1772	36
county commissioners to establish polling places	1773	36
Judges to be appointed; county clerk to notify; county clerk to give notice of election	1774	36
polls, time to be opened	1775	37
notice of election may be published in newspaper	1776	37
qualifications of electors	1777	37
ballot, form of	1778	38
candidates to be nominated by public meeting	1778	38
certificates of nomination to be filed with county clerk	1778	38
number of ballots to be published, booths to be provided	1778	38
how to be provided	1778	38
how to mark ballot	1778	40
challenge	1779	40
books to be kept by judges	1780	40
counting of ballots	1780	40
oaths to judges and trustees	1780	41
canvassing votes	1781	41
trustees elected to file oath of office	1782	41
who eligible to office of trustee	1783	41
registry precincts	1784	41
registry agents	1784	41
registry agents must take oath; office of registry agents, time and place of registering	1784	41
register, what to contain	1784	42
registry precincts, arrangement of	1785	42
register to be delivered to County Clerk	1785	43
expenses paid from school funds	1786	44
stationery, books and supplies	1786	44
compensation of registry agents	1786	44
bonds and compensation of school trustees	1787	44
financial statement of	1795	46
flag, must procure	1807	49
flag, must be displayed	1808	49
flag, expense of	1809	49
money, surplus used for building	1818	52
money, failure to pay over, felony	1817	52
money, received from sale of bonds, failure to pay over	1970	75
number of	1770	35
penalties	1800	48
pupils, must inquire into cases of those not attending school	1923	65
pupils, must appoint truant officer	1924	65
qualify, failure to	1782	41
qualifications	1770	35
removed, how	1982	76
tax, board must levy for interest	1813	51
term of	1770	35
vacancies, how filled	1980	75
VACANCIES—		
clerk of school district, in office of, how filled	1981	75
trustee, in office of, how filled	1980	75
trustees, removal and suspension of	1982	76